WHISPERS OF LIBERATION

Feminist Perspectives on the
New Testament

NICHOLAS KING

PAULIST PRESS
New York/Mahwah, N.J.

Scripture translations are made on the basis of the 27th edition of the Nestle-Aland Testamentum Graece, Deutsche Bibelgesellschaft, Stuttgart, 2d printing, 1994.

Cover design by James F. Brisson

Book design by Theresa M. Sparacio

Library of Congress Cataloging-in-Publication Data

King, Nicholas.
    Whispers of liberation : feminist perspectives on the New Testament /
Nicholas King.
        p. cm.
    Includes bibliographical references.
    ISBN 0–8091–3816–6 (alk. paper)
    1. Bible. N.T.—Criticism, interpretation, etc. 2. Bible. N.T.—Feminist criticism.
I. Title.
BS2379.K55   1998
225.6′082—dc21   98–35682
                                                                                              CIP

Published by Paulist Press
997 Macarthur Boulevard
Mahwah, New Jersey 07430

www.paulistpress.com

Printed and bound in the
United States of America

CONTENTS

SOCIIS IN CHRISTO IESU

INTRODUCTION

IN THE COURSE OF THE TWENTIETH CENTURY, and increasingly since the 1960s, people have become aware of a whole host of issues connected with the role of women in society and the ways in which they have been marginalized in male-dominated cultures. Virtually all the cultures that human history reveals to us are male-dominated, and most of the history that we know is written from the male point of view. It seems that we are being invited, as the present century draws to a close, to look again at the question of domination and subordination, not merely between the sexes, but also in all relationships among different groups and cultures in society.

One example of this is the question of the role of women in the Christian churches and, more specifically, the way that religious language can operate to keep women in an inferior position. At first sight this inferiority is an odd phenomenon in that although in most religions throughout history women seem to have constituted the majority of practicing believers, it is generally the men who have played the organizational roles. Many feminists believe this occurs because religion is a source of power, and men have traditionally taken on and clung to power.

This is not a problem peculiar to religious organizations, though. Most movements seem to have been dominated by men, at least on the organizational level. In saying that, I do not argue that it should be so; merely that it has been so. It may well be that the churches and non-Christian religious groups have been a step ahead of secular society in allowing women a prominent role. Nevertheless, we are dealing here with something of a puzzle, and in the view of many people, both men and women, a considerable scandal, given that Christianity claims to promote a gospel of freedom and a "discipleship of equals."

1

It cannot be denied that women have frequently been alienated and unchurched and that many women feel a great anger at the church even though they may stay within its boundaries. Therefore, a question poses itself with some urgency: What is the Spirit saying to the churches in the clamor of women to be recognized?

It occurred to me to write this book for a number of reasons. First, as a middle-aged celibate priest (of, I should judge, somewhat conservative disposition), I have become aware of the importance to me of the friendship of a number of women. At the same time, I have realized the extent to which I had been fearful of women—without precisely identifying the nature of that fear—and to some extent I suspect that is also true of the institutional church to which I belong. This in turn has given me an increasingly wider view of the ministry of women in the church. Slowly, I have come to realize the force of the feminist charge that the church has been grudging in its acceptance of what women have to offer.

Secondly, the gospels all attest that the women, including—according to the fourth gospel—the mother of Jesus, were at the crucifixion of Jesus. According to the synoptic gospels, the men had all disappeared in a panic. All the gospels agree that the women were the first to discover that Jesus' tomb was empty on Sunday morning and the first to be told that Jesus was risen. In Matthew and John, the first and fourth gospels, the women were the first to meet the risen Jesus. All agree that it was the women who were commissioned to be "apostles to the apostles." Then, however, the women disappear rather abruptly from any kind of leading role in the infant church, and it seemed to me that it would be interesting to know why.

Thirdly, while working in the troubled province of KwaZulu/Natal in the years after the historic South African elections, I became painfully aware of the aggressive postures adopted by many of our politicians, who were mostly male. Mainly in consequence of their persistently warlike utterances, each weekend alarming numbers of black Africans were killed under the pretext of a political struggle. In fact, politics was a cloak for many other interests: criminal activity, drug dealing, payment of old grudges and so on. Nevertheless, the killing raged on to the point where the deaths of fifty or sixty people over the weekend would merit no more than a paragraph tucked away on page three of the local newspaper. It occurred to me on several occasions that if our politics were in the hands of women, they would have more sense than to continue in this childishly lethal way. The fact is that KwaZulu/Natal is—to introduce a word that will make frequent appearance in this book—a patriarchal society. Patriarchal societies are , at their worst, dysfunctional. Because it is assumed that the head of the household has absolute rights and that "junior" members must do as they are told, any disagreement tends to be seen as an assault on the fabric of society and to be expressed violently and resisted with equal violence.

Fourthly, and partly in consequence of these last few factors, I conducted a seminar at St. Joseph's Theological Institute in Cedara, KwaZulu/Natal on women in the New Testament. Here the students, mainly black but also white, and mainly men but also women, argued and sweated over the texts. They taught me a great deal, much of which is in this book.

Finally, there was the heady discovery in April 1994 that the historic elections in South Africa were a liberation, not merely for black people, but also for white people. I was a "District Observer" for these elections and had the privilege of witnessing the miracle (that is not too strong a word) firsthand. This encouraged me to continue in the direction of rereading the Bible with new eyes and inviting others to do the same. I am certain that Scripture has on its agenda the liberation of all humanity, including both those who count as oppressed and those who count as oppressors. I came to realize there is nothing to fear in refusing to read the Bible in a way that oppresses or subjugates women. It is something to embrace as part of our own journey into freedom. It is not God, but human beings, who have willed the subjugation of one class of humanity to another, and therefore it is the God of freedom whom we shall encounter if we set forth on this journey. I am not saying anything new in this—the community of believers increasingly rejects the relegation of any class of human beings to an inferior category—but again and again I see in the life of the church and society evidence that the liberating message of the gospel—that all men and women are equal—needs to be proclaimed afresh. I do not suppose there shall ever be a moment this side of eternity when we shall be in a position to stop preaching this message, for human beings keep blundering into the view that the best way to stop feeling insecure is to find another human being, or group of people, upon whom they can look down.

For all these reasons, the general topic of "women in the New Testament" seemed an obvious one to pursue when the possibility of a sabbatical was suggested to me. The sabbatical was spent at Weston Jesuit School of Theology in Cambridge, Massachusetts, where the leisure given me to study in the awesome libraries there and the warmth and support of the Jesuit community at Faber House made the writing a pleasure. In addition, there were the stimulating New Testament colloquia run by Daniel Harrington, S.J., from which I learned a good deal, and the graduate seminar conducted by Professor Elisabeth Schüssler Fiorenza at Harvard Divinity School entitled "Gospel Stories of Wo/Men," which opened my eyes to the complexity of the issue. It is not just a matter of reading the particular texts: there are also hermeneutical questions of how one reads the text and how the texts were written.

Though this book is in touch with modern scholarship on the issue, it is not intended as a scholarly book. It is an introduction to some of the issues involved for all those interested in the questions of the role of women in society, in the church and in the Bible. Therefore, a caution should be prefixed: this book is not for those who are already at home in feminist readings of biblical texts, but is meant for those who are a little uneasy about feminism while feeling that there may be value in it.

It is a difficult issue that we are dealing with here. I am convinced that Scripture is the liberating word of God for all women and men, and that the church, the community of believers, is the place to find and interpret that Scripture. Nevertheless, I am also aware that for many intelligent and thoughtful and scholarly women of good will, the Bible and the church are seen as places of oppression. It is my belief that both the church and the Bible should function to set people free, and that this is the way in which the Spirit of God is calling us today. This book is therefore an attempt to see and help others to see how this may be so.

The first chapter tries to set out the nature of the problem. Chapter 2 tackles the difficult question of inclusive language, more to underline the difficulty than to answer the question. The third chapter looks briefly (more briefly than the subject deserves) at a few of the principal feminist biblical scholars in order to give the reader an idea of the range of thought involved. These three chapters, which some readers may find a bit tedious, are a necessary introduction to part 2 of the book, the examination of certain New Testament texts. What I shall be trying, quite explicitly, to do in part 2 is to show that it is possible to read these texts as a word of life for all, including some of the more difficult texts that we might be tempted to exclude from our Bible.

Some feminist scholars talk of the importance of reading Scripture with a "hermeneutics of suspicion," deliberately looking out for the conscious or unconscious codes whereby male authors or a male-dominated church inscribe the class interests of male domination into the text so that women (and others) are kept in what is deemed to be their place. I take, in contrast, a more deliberately optimistic approach to the text. I am not, that is to say, a "radical feminist," though in some sense of the word I count myself a feminist. My particular bias will lie in the direction of "saving the text," although that is not the only approach one could take.

Many feminists would reject my way of reading, and the reader must decide for himself or herself how to read the text. One observation may be appropriate here: feminist scholars speak a good deal of the importance of the "lens" or "window" through which one views the text of the Bible (or of any other piece of literature). By that they refer to the stance one takes in reading, which is very often dictated by one's own social location and past experience. Obviously it is important to be aware of one's own prejudice, but the result of this emphasis among some feminist scholars can occasionally be that they do not sufficiently look beyond the window itself to the view through the window, which is the text—that having concentrated on the "lens" through which the

Scripture is inspected, they have not really come to the full richness that is there in the pages of the Bible.

I am also aware that some reflective thinkers may object to my making this attempt on the grounds that I am a man. That, of course, cannot be helped.

It is worth noticing the possible objection that writing a book about women in, and feminist perspectives on, the New Testament has the same effect as writing on animals or cooking in the New Testament: it underscores the oddity of what one is talking about and confirms the marginalization of women as "other" and "different." I see the force of this argument, but believe that the nature of the issue makes the attempt worthwhile. At all events, I ask that you keep in mind the difficulty of the issue. This book does not really offer solutions. I am only trying to feel out the way ahead in a darkish place, whose obscurity poses something of a challenge to the authority of the church and of the Bible. I invite you, as you read chapters that look at particular texts, to join me in stretching out an uncertain hand into the dark, confident that there is a path ahead and that a hand will be outstretched in turn to meet us.

My thanks are due to those scholars and friends who generously took time to read some or all of the manuscript and saved me from many blunders. It is only fair to say that I did not always follow their advice, so they cannot be held responsible for the defects of this book. They include: Tom Brodie, O.P., (who gave me, among many other gifts, the suggestion of translating "Jews" as "Judaeans" in John 11), Judy Coyle, I.H.M., Heather Johnston, John Humphreys, S.J., Professor Alice Laffey, John McDade, S.J., Dr. Maxine Nurnberger, John O'Donnell, S.J., and the members of his seminar groups on the theology of the priesthood, Sue Rakoczy, I.H.M., Dr. Joan Taylor, Peg Tillery, the late Sister Cecilia Wilms and the biblical study group at the parish of St. Charles Borromeo in Woburn, Massachusetts, who taught me a great deal that is not to be found on library shelves. A great debt of gratitude is owed also to Kathleen Walsh, my editor at Paulist Press, whose sharp eye saved me from much foolish inconsequentiality. She cannot, of course, be blamed for any remaining foolish inconsequentialities.

The translations are my own. They are an important part of what this book is attempting to do. Sometimes I have been deliberately tendentious, in order to jolt the reader into looking at a familiar passage with fresh eyes. I think, however, that all translations I have adopted can be defended, even though some of them might not be appropriate for proclaiming in church. If some of the translations seem shocking, that may be because occasionally the New Testament ought to shock us.

This book is dedicated, with conscious ambiguity, both to my fellow Jesuits and to all those women and men, even those who are not explicitly Christian, who have helped me to glimpse what the companionship of Jesus Christ means and to dimly discern how to live out the exacting discipleship which that companionship entails.

Part I

CHAPTER ONE

IS THE "GOOD NEWS" REALLY
"BAD NEWS"?

THE BIBLE IS SUPPOSED TO BE "GOOD NEWS" for all humanity, a word of life for all people. If it turns out to be "bad news" for any section of the human race or the created world, then it is bad news for all of us. The feminist movement has for some time now been sending out alarm signals with regard to the collection of texts that we call the Bible, that it may be or can be employed in a way that is fundamentally hostile to women. Can that charge be made to stick? Is the feminist movement correct in this insight? It is an issue that deserves some further exploration.

There are, in fact, several "feminist movements," whose attitudes to the Bible vary from optimistic to hostile. Feminism, as we understand it at present, in one sense goes back to the nineteenth century. In another sense, it is the development of an awareness that started to appear in the 1960s in America and some parts of Europe and has appeared under many different forms since then. While some might argue that women have always had ways of asserting themselves against male oppression and so in that sense there has always been a women's resistance movement, never before has this truly operated as a movement nor been given the sophisticated theoretical articulation with which it is now presented. This very sophistication raises, however, a problem of which many feminists are aware: the "balkanization" of the movement. By this is meant the existence of several different forms of feminism that have somewhat different perspectives and aims and that might even seem to be at odds with each other. Another thing to keep in mind is that not all women consider themselves to be feminists. It is this issue that we now briefly address.

11

A) NOT ALL WOMEN ARE FEMINISTS

"You're not going to become one of these feminists, are you?" a woman friend, whom I have known for very many years, asked me in horror when I explained that I wanted to write something about the treatment of women in the New Testament. We did not have time to explore what she meant by the question, but it is clear that many women are appalled by the idea of feminism. That does not, of course, mean that feminism is mistaken, but it may mean that it has not expressed itself as well as it could. The objections to feminism are many and varied: "feminists are unfeminine and strident" would be one catchall expression of the prejudice that feminism sometimes arouses. It is, however, an expression of prejudice and needs to be faced as such. It is an excuse for not having to listen to what feminists are saying to us for fear that it might be true.

Another objection is that "feminists write such horrible English, in 'sociology-speak' with hyphenated multiplications of nouns and adjectives." There may be some truth to that charge, but, of course, it is not true of every feminist writer any more than it is true that the literary style of every male chauvinist is a model for imitation. The point here is that feminist writers try to make readers aware of how language operates: the way we use language often stems from unconscious presuppositions about relationships between the sexes.

A third charge laid against feminism is the fact that we have managed all this time without worrying about the alleged oppression of women, so "why now, all of a sudden?" The answer to that question could simply be that now is the time when the Spirit seems to be stimulating our consciences to address the problem. After all, we are sometimes extraordinarily slow to grasp the implications of the gospel, especially where the implications seem to be at war with our own self-interest.

It was only during the nineteenth century, in Europe and America, at any rate, that Christians felt seriously compelled to do anything about slavery. In our time no one, except for the seriously deranged, would go on television and argue that slavery is a "good thing," and that it is really in the interests of the slaves because that is the way God has made them. One may argue that Christians have taken their time in getting around to this position, but they have gotten there. Even though our world is still marred by the fact of slavery, no one will nowadays seek to justify it as the will of God, or as "the way things ought to be." We are often slow to see injustice when there is a danger that our comfort may be thereby affected. Just as with the issue of slaves in the last century, so as we come to the end of the present century, we are being invited to examine anew the treatment that men, including Christian men in positions of leadership, have meted out to women.

Some may question, "But what is wrong with men's treatment of women?" The underlying implication is that there is no problem, and that was presumably what underlay my friend's slightly aggressive nervousness that I might be turning into one of "these feminists." The question of the relationship of men to women, whether posed generally or more specifically, as this book poses it, about how the Bible, in particular the "New" or "Second" Testament, functions within that relationship, needs to be addressed. The issues that feminist readers of the Bible have raised are just not going to go away, and I should like to outline some of them at this point. Others will emerge in the course of subsequent chapters.

b) Ways of Reading the Bible

At this point, let me make an observation that is fundamental to the whole enterprise on which this book is engaged, namely, that reading the Bible is a more complex activity than we tend to suppose. There is a science called hermeneutics, which looks at the question of how we manage to communicate anything at all to each other, how we succeed in "meaning." There is no one way of doing hermeneutics, but for our purposes it may be sufficient for me to say that communication of any kind is not quite so simple as it seems.

For example, you might imagine that all I have to do is write down on the page what I want to say, and all you have to do is read it. That is the commonsense view, but common sense can lead us astray. There is the complication that I may not have put onto the page precisely what I wanted to say, and you might not have fully grasped the meaning of my words; and if you do not know any English at all, then what is going on is something quite different again.

The situation is even more complicated when it comes to the Bible. First of all, the Bible was not written in English, but in at least three other languages. Second, we cannot be absolutely sure of the original text in some cases. Third, the authors lived in situations and cultures very different from our own. Fourth, if we are dependent on translation into our own language, there is yet another barrier between us and the original. Fifth, some modern theorists of communication do not believe that it makes sense to speak of "truth" in a document, only of "marks on a page." For them, truth is defined by the community that produces or receives a document, and is not something absolute. That is obviously problematic for the Bible, whose readers look to it very often precisely for some "copper-bottomed truths" in a shifting and insecure world. Biblical hermeneutics is a rather tricky enterprise; and feminist biblical hermeneutics, which is what we are looking at in this book, is even more so.

c) A Man's World—Three Useful Terms

Feminist biblical scholars ask us to notice that we live in what is still a "man's world." The Bible is a part of that world, and it has often been used in the interests of keeping things that way. Feminist scholars, in exploring this point, have relied upon a specific vocabulary. Terms such as *androcentric, patriarchal* and *kyriarchal,* which I will introduce below, are of importance in examining the questions that underlie this book, and we shall have frequent occasion to use them in the course of it.

i) Androcentric

This term means "from the male point of view." Its opposite, meaning "from the female point of view," is *gynecentric* or *gynaikocentric.* The term *androcentric* is applied to the Bible insofar as the dominant angle on persons and events is the man's rather than the woman's. Many feminist scholars will argue that the collection of texts which we call the Bible is strongly marked by androcentrism.

ii) Patriarchal

The word *patriarchal* refers to a view of society or a society of a particular kind in which the male head of the household owns everything, including individual people, wives, children, extended family, slaves, animals and land. In a patriarchal society, the male can, therefore, do what he will with his "possessions," including selling them, and has the right to punish individuals by methods up to and including capital punishment.

Feminist scholars argue that many injustices, in the church as well as in society at large, that are still with us today, are the direct consequences of the absolute authority conferred on men by a patriarchal society. Other analysts take a slightly different line and argue that certain kinds of societies, including some of the cultures represented in the New Testament, require this concentration of power in the person of the patriarch if they are to survive at all. While that may be so, the problem for Christians comes when the patriarchal norms that belong only to a particular society, in its own time and context, are interpreted as the will of God, binding for all times and all cultures. This is a problem because, if patriarchy inevitably leads to injustice (which many feminist thinkers would argue), then God is proclaimed as a God who wills injustice.

iii) Kyriarchy and Kyriocentric

The word *kyriarchy* and its close relative *kyriocentric* have to do with the Greek word *kyrios*, which means "Lord." The term is known to many of us from the Greek of the old Tridentine mass in the vocative form, as in *Kyrie Eleison*. In that sense it is often used to refer to Jesus in the New Testament, and to refer to God in the Old. It can also mean the male head of house, and you can see how easily the one can be assimilated into the other, so that the Christian desire to assign "Lordship" to Jesus Christ can be used to bolster an "over-lordship" of other males as the will of God. *Kyriarchy,* then, is the rule of the "lords," those who are in positions of power and domi-nance in societies and cultures; and *kyriocentric* would describe any-thing written from their point of view.

The problem, therefore, is that if the Bible (and, to be fair, most of the texts, both ancient and modern, that are known to us) simply presents the male world and the masculine point of view as norma-tive, then women and the feminine point of view are on the periph-ery. Where the male is at the center, women are "different" or "other"; where the man is the norm, women are often invisible. It is worth spending some time on this concept because it is at the heart of the problems that feminists have with reading the Bible, and we shall meet this issue over and over again.

d) THE FEMINIST APPROACH TO THE TEXTS

Many people, women as well as men, find it difficult to see the point of all this. But consider the closely linked ideas that European and North American society (the "kyriarchy") has held until quite recently with regard to the appropriate treatment of slaves and people of other races. In our day people would get quite uncomfort-able if I were to argue that "slaves are an inferior class of people, whom God has appointed to be in that state" or that "blacks must learn to know the place that God has ordained for them. They must live together and emerge from their God-given homelands only to serve us whites." A familiar doctrine, apartheid, as it is known in the country where I work, is wholly discredited today, at least in theory, and quite appropriately reviled.

What those views on slavery and on the status of black people have in common is the belief that a class or classes of people ("them") are inferior to other classes ("us"), and as such may be exploited. This is precisely, feminists would argue, the doctrine that androcentric patri-archy has invoked in order to keep women "in their place." Their con-cern is to ensure that this doctrine is not applied to the Bible and its

interpretation—that is, that the Bible is not used to maintain patriarchy. If the Bible is all about maintaining patriarchy, then, the argument goes, women can have no more to do with it than can black
people read a Bible that is used to justify apartheid.

Feminist thinkers have many different ways of reading the Bible, but
all of these approaches have at least three aspects in common: they are
partisan, committed to action and holistic. These three aspects may
help to indicate the way in which feminists, in interpreting the texts,
are doing something that may be new and unfamiliar and may serve to
explain why their manner of argument may seem foreign to us.

i) Feminist Biblical Scholarship Is Partisan

Feminist scholarship expressly and deliberately sets itself against
the "value-free" and "impartial" approach to biblical scholarship
that regarded itself as something akin to a science. The feminist
approach is partisan, consciously and explicitly looking at the text
from the point of view of women, and especially of those women
who, in consequence of the way the world is run, find themselves at
the margins of society, those who are poor and without resources.
These people are—such is the way of our world—often nonwhite
women and women from the lower income groups.

Feminist scholars would claim that the older, "impartial" way of
reading the Bible was also partisan, that it consciously or unconsciously expressed the values of the dominant class, the kyriarchy.
Sometimes feminists will use the metaphor of the "lens" through
which they gaze at the world to explain this understanding of biblical
interpretation. They acknowledge and are aware that they have a
"lens," a partisan way of looking at reality. Feminist thinkers would
claim that the same is true for everyone—everyone has such a lens,
even if she or he is not explicitly aware of it. Recognizing this aspect of
feminist biblical readings is essential and may urge the reader to
examine his or her own "lens" or bias. If you find yourself saying, "But
my reading of the Bible is objective and value-free," then look again.

Understanding that feminist Bible reading concentrates on the
"lens" may also help to solve a problem that many readers are

uneasy with when they encounter feminist exegesis for the first time. Characteristically, they express this problem by saying that the feminist way of reading Scripture is very praiseworthy, but life is not quite so simple as it suggests, and that things look rather different in the nonideal situation of the "real world." That is the effect of the lens; it brings certain (perhaps hitherto neglected) features of the text into uncomfortably sharp relief.

ii) Feminist Biblical Scholarship Is Committed to Action

The second aspect of feminist bible reading is that it is explicitly committed to praxis. This is a Greek word, of which Aristotle made great use, meaning "action." In recent literature, however, it has been given a Marxist coloring and means not just action, but the unending cycle of action and reflection on the world in which we live in order to transform it and put an end to oppression.

This is quite different from the way many were trained, from what would be considered the "older" and more traditional way of reading the Bible, what feminist scholars would call the "dominant exegesis of the kyriarchy." In that approach, there was a sense of scripture scholars working in a vacuum, like white-coated scientists who split the atom but gave no thought to the consequences of the power they had released. The "scientific method" was used to find the "objective meaning" of the text, and even if the text were the Sermon on the Mount, one could still be a good interpreter of the text regardless of whether or not one's life conformed to the gospel. The feminist approach to the biblical text will not allow that kind of a wedge to be driven between our reading of the New Testament and the way we conduct our lives or organize the world.

iii) Feminist Biblical Scholarship Sees Creation as a Whole

Thirdly, feminist biblical scholarship embraces the whole of creation in explicit solidarity. Obviously this will include women in solidarity with each other, but it will also include solidarity with all those who are oppressed by the "dominant kyriarchy." So Blacks, Latin Americans, Arabs, Jews, Asians and anyone else who might be oppressed because they belong to a discernible class that is not the dominant one, such as those who are disabled or homosexual, can be the objects of feminist solidarity. Equally, if any of those groups should present themselves as oppressors of another group, they too can be the targets of feminist criticism. Nor does it end with people, for feminism includes also care for the environment. You will therefore find environmentally inclined women ("ecofeminists") critically examining the claims that the Bible empowers the human race to exploit created nature for its own purposes, regardless of the consequences.

Still other feminists, meanwhile, fight against anti-Judaism. This includes the often unnoticed anti-Judaism that defends the New Testament against charges of chauvinism by comparing it (favorably) with its Jewish background, which, for the purpose, is taken to be more hostile to women. That move in defense of the gospels tends to support the kind of belief system whereby Christians have, down the centuries, justified the oppression of Jews. And feminism is opposed to *all* oppression, of whatever kind, even the oppression of men as men.

E) THE FEAR OF FEMINISM

It seems to me improbable that all readers would without further ado call themselves feminists, and I can imagine a few possible readers who would strongly resist if they thought they might be so labeled. What is the cause of this resistance?

Some feminists will argue that it is a question of power. Men resist the feminist analysis because they are fearful of losing power, and women resist it because their best chance of a slice of the action is if they stay close to the powerful males, which means supporting the status quo. It is probably not as simple as that, though this analysis should prompt all of us to examine whether we share some of the resistance to feminism and, if so, for what reasons.

i) Fear of the Loss of Power

Sometimes the resistance comes simply from the fact that men fear women, but there are other kinds of fear that may be operative as well. Sometimes unconsciously, these fears influence the way in which we deal with questions of this sort. There is, first, the fear that my comfortable existence may be turned upside down if I subscribe to the feminist analysis. At root, this is a fear about loss of power. Even if we do not feel particularly powerful, we may unconsciously mark out our territory, using the "givens" of the world we know; and if suddenly the role of women is to be less confined than we had previously supposed it to be, our power base crumbles and our securities vanish. Some men panic at this prospect because of the sense that women are invading "their" territory, and some women are equally uncertain as the field of operations suddenly becomes unfamiliarly extensive.

An analogy is suggested by our experience in South Africa, where, before apartheid finally came to an end, many of the reservations expressed by whites at the possibility of being governed by black people seemed to be rooted, not so much in an objection to black people as such, but in the perception that the world was turning upside down and they did not really know what things would look like after the transformation, nor how much control they would have left. And indeed some black people were equally bemused at the prospect of an integrated government.

ii) Fear in Defense of the Bible

Another kind of fear, for religious people, is the panic at the prospect that the Bible, "which I thought I knew and loved," may turn out to be something rather different from what we supposed. We like our landmarks to remain landmarks. If they turn into something else, we are uncomfortable, feeling as if we do not know where it will all end. Some of us may have a lurking anxiety that the way we have been reading the Bible may turn out not to be based upon unselfishness or generosity as we had supposed. The fears generated by the feminist analysis of Scripture may, in part, have to do with the prospect that it may require a complete revision of our views of Scripture. If, as the feminist critique would hold, the whole collection of texts in the Old and New Testaments is really written only from the androcentric point of view and are serving the function of installing as unassailable the rights of the dominant male, then in what sense can the Bible possibly be the Word of God?

iii) How to Cope with Our Fears

All human beings have a craving for security, and the fears that I have outlined here are all responses to insecurity. Ultimately, however, that security can be found only in the mystery whom we call God. Indeed, some feminists print that word as *G-d,* to preserve the mystery (rather as for Jews the sacred name of God is to be written in consonantal form as *YHWH,* and never to be pronounced), and to make it clear that the mystery is not at the service of our comfortable prejudices.

It may be that we need to go into the darkness in order to find what we thought we already knew and loved. We already did know and love it of course; but we human beings need constantly to be reminded that God (or G*d/G-d) cannot be explained or domesticated. The insights of the feminist movement may be simply an invitation from God to let go of elements in our understanding of reality that are not God, divine though we may suppose them to be.

The questions raised by modern feminists will, I suggest, turn out to be no more destructive of the Bible than the apparent problem raised by the work of sixteenth-century scientists like Galileo and Copernicus, or the research of Darwin in the nineteenth century. In all these cases there appeared to be a real danger that the Bible would be discredited, but that has not turned out to be the case. Instead, what has happened is that we have discovered more about what the Bible really is, and in what sense it can be said to be true. From this distance we can see that the way to handle it is not to resist those who lead the new intellectual movements, for they may be doing what God has asked of them. Rather, our approach must be to grow into a more mature understanding of what we mean when we say that the Bible is a sacred text. If we feel a bit disoriented, that does not necessarily mean that things have gone wrong.

God is always beyond anything that we could possibly grasp; and therefore at least sometimes on our journey toward God we must expect to find ourselves in unfamiliar territory, with no map and precious few recognizable landmarks. If we never have that experience, then we shall forever be falling into the all-too-human temptation of creating a familiar (and therefore much safer) "God in our own image and likeness." That fantasy God will not, however, be identical with the real God, the one who alone can lead us into life and freedom.

Conclusion: Why Bother at All?

One might think that if the examination of feminist claims is as difficult a procedure as indicated, then I might be well advised not to bother and to pursue instead some other form of academic enterprise. My reasons for undertaking this study are explained in the introduction, but since at times in the course of writing this book the whole thing seemed an impossible or radically unsettling task, I may as well attempt another answer at this point.

Not long ago, I was told the following story representative of the rivalry among the various religious orders: a Benedictine, a Dominican and a Jesuit went to play golf, but were warned at the clubhouse that the foursome playing ahead of them might be very slow, as they were visually impaired, and in fact legally blind. The Benedictine exclaimed in awe at their spiritual courage; the Dominican started to compose a sermon on "spiritual blindness"; while the Jesuit stubbed out his cigar and exclaimed, "Why can't they play at night?" Now I laughed a good deal at that, and reflected afterwards that this may have been because the story came uncomfortably close to home.

When we are first faced with a group that is "different," our first reaction, until we know them as people, and learn to share their aspirations, is very often "Why can't they be like us?" or "Why do we have to see them being so different?" I have a friend, a fellow Jesuit, who is completely deaf, but who lip-reads to perfection. At first it seems odd, and can be irritating, in our fast-quipping sound-bite society, to have to pause and make sure that one is facing him in order to make sure that he can understand what I am saying, but the tiny effort involved is more than amply repaid, and I am frequently moved by watching him communicate with other people in sign language.

We tend to instinctively regard our own experience as "normal," and that can cut us off from the riches offered by people who are different from us. If we take the trouble to see reality through other "lenses," it may at first be a struggle, and we may even need to have the sense that we are doing something rather noble. But gradually something else happens, and we realize that we are being enriched more than we could have imagined. It is in the search for that richness through diversity that I have found the courage to continue writing this book.

CHAPTER TWO

"THE CHILD OF PERSON"—
DOES INCLUSIVE LANGUAGE
REALLY MATTER?

INCLUSIVE LANGUAGE TRIES TO AVOID SPEECH that places particular groups of people on the margin of society's interests. Therefore, for example, we do not these days talk about the "disabled," but about the "other-abled," or the physically or mentally challenged, and we prefer to describe groups by their own preferred self-designation, such as "African American" instead of "Black." By the same token, it is nowadays impolite to talk of "mankind" when we mean men and women, and it is considered better not to speak of "God Himself," since God is neither male nor female. In both these cases, women are left feeling excluded and unable to identify with the designation; and it is no good our saying that we do not *intend* their exclusion. If a large population feels excluded by traditional language, then we must examine the way we talk and write.

This tendency to change the language we use produces, of course, a reaction, and you are no doubt familiar with the rather defensive old jokes against the idea of inclusive language; the "Child of Person" referred to in the title of this chapter is one of the least imaginative, a parody of the "politically correct" version of the gospel phrase "Son of Man"; and there are ostensibly witty asides about visiting a town in the north of England called "Personchester," the activity of "womanipulation," and so on. The interesting thing about these jokes is less in their effect on their targets than in what they reveal about the teller. They express the discomfort and sometimes latent anger generated by the prospect of a change that they have not controlled.

In this chapter I should like to do three things: (1) attempt to explain why the question of language seems important, especially in the religious sphere; (2) explore whether it is possible to change our language about God; and (3) examine whether we *need* to make such a change.

Three remarks may serve to point up the difficulty of this topic. First, it is quite possible to become verbally very adroit at using inclusive language and still operate in such a way as to keep women marginalized. Even if we succeeded in solving the problem that we are considering in this chapter of how we are to talk and write, it would be only a beginning of a solution to the key question of how we are to behave, for exclusive language is symptomatic of a more profound ailment in our society.

Second, we have to admit that while *man* until fairly recently was a useful term to apply to all humanity—a strong-sounding monosyllable that functioned well in a variety of sentences—it has changed its meaning, largely under pressure from feminist thinkers. It no longer means what it used to mean, to a point where it would now be discourteous to use the term or its plural if the intended referent is the whole of humanity. We cannot simply rely on what is linguistically easy or useful.

A third point is a theological one that touches on the mystery of the divine. We do not know, in a sense, precisely what we are talking about when we are talking to or of God, for God is a mystery about which we are permanently unable to talk successfully. That being the case, we cannot make the deceptively simple move of appealing to the language of the Bible to help solve the problem, because the Bible is written in the language of its time, and biblical translations use the conventions of the age in which they were composed. Words, as I have indicated, change their meanings, and unless we recognize this fact, we may end up saying something quite different from what we intended to say.

From all the above it follows that we should not expect to solve the problem of appropriate language in this chapter. On the other hand, there is nothing at all to be gained from pretending that the problem does not exist. It will take at least a generation for us to feel our way toward new methods of translating biblical and liturgical texts, for the issues are complex, and their resolutions are bound to cause pain and to take much hard work. That, however, does not entitle us to shrug our shoulders and move on to something else. Were we to do that, we might be resisting the invitation of God. If today women feel hurt and alienated by what they experience when they go to church, then that is a serious issue and must be dealt with.

A) THE IMPORTANCE OF LANGUAGE

Many people stir restively when the matter of inclusive language arises, and they ask why it matters so much how one talks about God and about human beings. The truth is that language is not just an arbitrary series of signs, nor is it something that can never change. The way we talk has an important influence on how we think about the world; language has an extraordinary amount to do with power.

In the film *The Silence of the Lambs,* one of the most chilling moments was made so in large part by the dialogue between the serial killer and the woman he was holding captive at the bottom of an empty well. When he commanded her to do things, such as place her empty plate in a basket so that it could be hauled to the top of the well, the man did not use the imperative ("put the plate in the basket") or a politer form ("please put the plate in the basket"), but the neuter indicative: "it puts its plate in the basket." This mangling of the grammar of the sentence revealed the ghastliness of what was going on. Language is important and expresses the relationships that people have with one another.

The kind of language that we use in addressing God or referring to God or to the situation of the human race before God is important. And many people are today uncomfortable with the kind of language that suggests that God is in some way masculine. One reason for that is, as Mary Daly has expressed it with lapidary succinctness, that "if God is male, then the male is God." It is for this reason that some have suggested gender-neutral words like "God/ess," which is better in print than in conversation, or with a pleasing Anglo-Saxon sound, "Womangod," and its near relative to describe the human race, "Wo/man." Some like the sound of "Godself" to avoid a genderized pronoun. It is, however, dangerously easy to parody these uses, and so pretend that they are about something unimportant, evading the serious point that they make.

The serious point can be expressed in another way, which I tried with a seminar of largely black, largely male students, some of whom were resistant to the feminist critique of language. I asked them what it would be like if in every text of the liturgy or the Bible where "men" is used to refer to the whole human race one were to substitute "whites," so that the Creed would have Jesus coming down "for us and for all whites" and the Lord's Prayer would start in Zulu, "Mlungu wethu osezulwini" ("Our White Man who are in Heaven"). They saw the point. And the point is a simple one—those who worship at our liturgy should not feel excluded by the language that is used so that they become the "Invisible Other."

Language *is* important. You can only speak (of God or of anything else) in the language that you have, but language changes all the time, and that adds to the difficulty. The issue is further compounded when it is God that is being talked about, for attempting to speak of God means that we are forced to batter at the walls of language.

b) Can We Change the Language We Use about God?

For a while now, people have announced the demise of religion. Its obstinate refusal to die, however, points to the power it exercises. If language is also powerful, then in talking about religious language we are swimming in very deep waters. Some people suggest that it is simply impossible to change the language that feminists find so offensive, such as calling God *He/Him,* and argue that the normal term to cover all of humanity is *man.* But language, including the terms in which the revelation of God is expressed, is changing all the time under social and cultural pressures of various kinds.

The language of what we call the Old Testament is mainly, though not entirely, Hebrew, but our Jewish forebears also used materials that had been written in other languages (such as the

Babylonian account of creation, or bits from the Wisdom tradition of Egypt) to fashion the picture of God that they present to us in the Scriptures. Similarly, Jesus preached and taught in Aramaic, his native language. Although he and some in his circle may have known Greek, it was probably the remarkable figure of Paul who first "translated" that preaching out of Aramaic into Greek, the language of the Mediterranean world. Therefore there is nothing fixed about any of the "original" languages in which the Bible was written; God's revelation was passed on in the language appropriate to the time and place in which it was being heard. A century or more after the gospel was proclaimed in Greek, it became necessary to translate it into Latin, the language of the western half of the Mediterranean and of North Africa. Latin was the language in which I heard the word proclaimed in the mass during my formative years. Like many of my age or a bit older, I well remember thinking with some excitement (and quite incorrectly) that I was actually hearing the words of Jesus himself, once I knew enough Latin to know what was going on.

From the late Middle Ages onwards, the Scriptures were with increasing frequency translated into the vernacular languages. In English the King James Version, with its sonorous cadences, came to dominate, and it has largely shaped the English language as it was spoken, at least until the last third of the present century. After a little over three centuries, that version seems incredibly settled. Indeed, it is quite clear that many people, consciously or unconsciously, regard it as God's own words, rather as I supposed with the Latin I heard as a boy. So, for example, simply starting a sentence with the "Thou shalt not" of sixteenth-century English can make it sound incontrovertible and invested with divine authority. Tradition is extraordinarily important in our journey towards God, for it keeps us in touch with the community that has worshiped God down the ages. If, however, tradition becomes a defense against the invitation of God, then it is no longer a help on the road, but an idol to be torn down. The Bible is a fundamental part of our tradition, but it is dangerously possible for us to use it as a shield against uncomfortable change.

c) Do We Really *Need* to Change Our Language?

Why go to the trouble of making changes in this revered collection of texts that we call the Bible? The short answer is that given the evolution of our language, it no longer means exactly what it used to mean. Consider, for example, the following lines translated from Psalm 8:

> what is man that you remember him?
> And the Son of Adam that you care for him? (Ps 8:4)

What, in our time, does that say to women?

What about the songs sung in Exodus 15, thought by many Hebrew scholars to include the oldest poetry in the Old Testament, which read in part:

> YHWH is a man of war...
> Sing to YHWH because he has triumphantly triumphed. . .
> the horse and its rider he has thrown in the sea. (Ex 15:1–3).

How might someone, especially a woman or a pacifist, pray their way through that?

Or look at Exodus 19:15:

> and he said to the people...'do not touch a woman.'

Notice that this is said at the moment when Israel is gathering before its God to receive the covenant. Two things are evident: First, it is clear that women are not included in the invitation, at the most significant moment in Israel's history; and second, the women are seen as liable to prevent the men from gaining access to the holiness of God. It is certainly appropriate to enter various anthropological explanations of why this is found in the text as it stands, but if today women feel excluded or marginalized in consequence of the ancient beliefs that underlie the text, then we have a problem.

It is not simply a matter of the Bible. There is also a problem with regard to our liturgical texts, which are profoundly influenced by the language of the First and Second ("Old" and "New") Testaments. I come up against this each day when reciting the

office. The breviary used by Catholic priests is an assortment of biblical texts, mainly psalms, but there are also nonbiblical texts there,
such as hymns and prayers of intercession for various classes of
people. Hymns could be subjected to an analysis all of their own,
but consider, from the feminist point of view, a perspective already
sensitive to the problem of inclusive language, the following
excerpts from the "bidding prayers" (written, be it noted, in the last
thirty years) with which morning and evening prayer ends each day,
remembering that a response is repeated after each intercession:

*We give thanks to Christ...because he was not ashamed to call us his
brothers.*

Response: Lord Jesus, we are your brothers.

...so that men may know through us...your love.

*Teach us to see you present in all men....(Wednesday Week 1, Morning
Prayer)*

*Christ became man to make us sons of God, and he intercedes for us
before God our Father. (Saturday Week 1, Morning Prayer)*

The will of Christ is for all men to be saved....

*Response: Draw all men to yourself, Lord. (Monday Week 3, Evening
Prayer)*

Blessed are the peacemakers...they are indeed the sons of God.

*Response: Your Kingdom come, O Lord. (Tuesday Week 4, Evening
Prayer)*

*It is the Father's will that men should see him in the face of his beloved
Son.*

Let us honor him....

You are the hope and joy of men in every age....

May Christ's coming renew [the Church's] youth and vigor in the service of men.... (Thursday Week 4, Morning Prayer)

These are simply examples of how insensitive our language can be. You can certainly find other such examples. The issue we are confronting was hardly visible when these prayers were written thirty years ago, and the writers are not to be blamed for not having seen it then. The question is, what are we to do about it and how are we to respond to it now?

This is not a particularly easy question to answer. It must be conceded that the problem starts with the Bible itself, which feeds much of our liturgical language. The authors of the Scriptures seem to have been male, and the Bible's outlook is androcentric. Moreover it is patriarchal, for its authors generally assume a view of society in which the male father of the household is in charge and dominant. It also tends to be kyriarchal, at least in the sense that the sympathy of biblical authors tends to be with those whom you might call the establishment (although there are other tendencies at work in the Bible).

In addition, the biblical images for God tend to err in the direction of the masculine and authoritarian (as we have seen in the examples above) rather than the feminine or consensual, and the grammatical gender of God is invariably masculine. To some extent this is unavoidable; in the languages in which the Bible was written, principally Hebrew and Greek, but also a certain amount of Aramaic, the author has always to make a choice about grammatical gender. In practice, this meant that God invariably had the masculine gender in Hebrew. The reason for this is that many of the biblical authors were cautious to resist what they saw as Canaanite polytheism. In the Canaanite pantheon, there were a good many goddesses, and if a Hebrew author were to construct a sentence that referred to, for example, "God Herself," they might be accused of undermining their monotheism. So it was almost inevitable that God would function grammatically as masculine.

It would be simpler if the Bible had originally been written in the languages of Southern Africa, such as Zulu or Sesotho, which do not demand that kind of grammatical distinction. The word for a "person" in these languages can refer to either a man or a woman, and the words for God carry no implication about gender. However, the Bible was not written in those languages, a fact which allows some to argue that "the Bible talks about God as male, so we should do the same."

Yet, the authors of the Bible held a good many views that we no longer hold, such as the earth being flat or the sun going around the earth. And there are plenty of Old Testament injunctions that Christians choose to ignore, such as keeping the annual festival of booths (Deuteronomy 16:16), or stoning adulterers (Deuteronomy 22:22), putting towns to the sword (e.g., Joshua 8:1–29) or slaughtering the Red Heifer (Numbers 19:4).

Still, though, it would be possible for traditionally minded opponents to argue that the Bible reveals to us something about God, including the way we speak about God. They might further argue that we speak of biblical texts as "the word of the Lord" and that the Lord would not allow the Bible to mislead us. As a matter of fact, though, people are frequently misled by the Bible, such as those who, in South Africa, gave apartheid a biblical justification, or people (increasing in number as the century and millennium come to a close) who with absolute confidence give us the date when the world will end.

Indeed, very often you will find that people in fact mean by "the Bible" nothing other than the King James Version (or some other influential translation) that was read to them as children. They would not for a second consider that the Hebrew original might have a superior claim, or perhaps they would argue that the King James is a faithful rendition of the original. While it is in some ways, no translation is ever perfect. The committee that produced that much loved version, for all their impressive scholarship, certainly made mistakes. A further issue to consider is the fact that language, as we have said before, changes its meaning. The sixteenth-century English prose does not mean quite the same thing now as it did then, and we cannot cling, without any further ado, to the translation that has been hallowed by antiquity.

Moreover, if the Spirit of God has in our century invited us to become more aware of the suffering and marginalization of women caused by the inequities of our society, then to continue to parrot the old language simply because it is old may lead us into infidelity to that call of the Spirit. Therefore, we have reached a crisis point with regard to our translations of the Bible and with regard to the language that we use in the liturgy. The question is: What can we do about it?

d) Three Ways of Coping with the Crisis

There are three possibilities, not necessarily exclusive, for dealing with the issue of inclusive language.

i) Changing Language about God

The first possibility entails changing the language about God. This means that God is referred to as "she" as well as "he," and "Father" is alternated with "Mother." "Man" would only be employed when a male is referred to, using the various circumlocutions ("they," "people," "humans," "person," "one," "he/she," and so forth as context and eloquence permit) that have been developed in recent years. This would not be particularly easy to manage, but it is surprising how adroit one can become with a little practice; certainly the discipline of attempting it is an excellent one.

Some feminists point to the fact that in many Christian traditions liturgies start with the invocation of the triune formula, "In the name of the Father, and of the Son, and of the Holy Spirit," which can leave them feeling from the outset that they don't really belong in this patriarchal mindset. This is especially so if the third member of the Trinity is referred to as "he," as is characteristically the case. So what is one to do about that?

ii) Looking for Feminine Images of God

There are other and deeper problems involved in the feminist approach to the Bible than merely the grammatical gender of pronouns and possessive adjectives. A second strategy involves considering the issue of images for God. If God is presented as "a warrior and a man of war," or if the kinds of things that God is imaged as doing are exclusively masculine activities, then the call to women to hear the voice of this God may be somewhat dulled. Therefore, a second approach must involve the quarrying of the Bible for images that are appropriate for women as well as men. The point of this is to strike a balance, not to lay the groundwork for the argument that "God is a woman." God is neither a woman nor a man, or rather, God is both woman and man, for we are all created in the image and likeness of God. Since, however, it tends to be the masculine features of God that predominate in our liturgical and biblical speech, it seems proper to redress the imbalance by making imaginative use of the places in Scripture (admittedly a minority of biblical passages) where God is described in feminine terms. This might also encourage a broadening of the selections of Scripture offered in the lectionary.

We might, for example, cite the beautiful maternal images in Hosea 11:3–4:

> It was I who taught Ephraim to walk, I took them up in my arms...I led them with cords of human kindness, with bands of love. I was to them like those who lift infants to their cheeks. I bent down to them and fed them,...

which clearly expresses the motherhood of God. We could also consider the image of the banquet in Isaiah 25:6 ff, taken up later in the Book of Revelation (21:4), where

> the Lord God will wipe away tears from all faces,

which combines God's rather masculine "Lordship" with an undeniably maternal gesture and so relativizes both ideas. There are several useful images of this sort in Isaiah 40–55, the chapters written for the exiled community of Israel in Babylon, who after half a century of retribution and as the time for their return drew near, perhaps needed a gentler picture of God than the punishing Judge that Jeremiah had offered them in the years leading up to their exile. So God is spoken of as

...like a woman in labor,... (42:14)

and the servant of God as one who does not

...break the bruised reed, or quench the dimly burning wick.
(42:3)

At 49:15 the charge that God has forgotten the exiles is dismissed in
the following remarkable image:

Can a woman forget her nursing child, or show no compassion for
the child of her womb?

That is not the whole story, of course; for the poet-prophet com-
pares God to a husband in chapter 54, and in chapter 47 allows himself a horribly vindictive address to the enemy Babylon, considered
precisely as woman. Nevertheless, if we can recall the circumstances
in which these poems were penned, we may be able to find here
some useful suggestions as to how our language can evolve.

There are possibilities in the New Testament as well. God is compared to a woman who celebrates after finding the missing drachma,
a tenth of her total wealth (Luke 15:8–10), and to a baker woman
(Matthew 13:33). The essential thing is to use what is there in the
Bible in order to listen more attentively to God's self-revelation and to
notice that in order to do so we may have to make a deliberate effort
to bring these images to the surface.

Yet, there are far more images for God in both the Old and the
New Testaments that stress God's male attributes than there are
images that bring out God's feminine qualities. This is simply the
product of the context in which the biblical writers lived and of the
culture for which they wrote. The Bible, therefore, as many feminist
scholars have remarked, is androcentric and patriarchal beyond our
power of remedy. We can tamper with the surface sound, but the
underlying structure will continue to represent a world in which the
male perspective was dominant. If this is the case, then the choice is
between abandoning the Bible on the grounds that it has nothing to
say to women and staying with it because there are whispers of liberation in it for all who are oppressed. Some women have opted for

the first course; but many have not because the Bible remains a part of who they are or because they find there the words that set people free. Thus they still find hope in the text. What can we say to encourage them?

iii) Uncomfortably Leaving Things As They Are

This leads us to the third possibility—that the text is left the way it is and is allowed to jar on our awakened sensibilities, so that when we read of "God Himself" we make the subversive response "Yes, but...." This solution accepts the biblical texts as products of their time and community, and allows them to prod us into a divine discomfort. As far as possible, that is to say, we shall make the alterations that will be necessary in order to bring female images into view and downplay the excessively male picture of God, but we shall also accept the text just as it is and work with it.

In canvassing this possibility, I am not arguing that we must not interfere with the Bible. Clearly that is not the case, or we should hold to every prescription in the Book of Leviticus, such as the list of unclean animals in chapter 11 or the instruction on male impurity in 15:2–18. We should by the same token include every verse of the Bible in our lectionary, even the more blush-making sections of the Song of Songs. So we are, to some degree, at ease with the idea of selecting bits from Scripture and rejecting others. This is what happens, for example, when someone says, "I don't like St. Paul" or dismisses the Letter of James as "an epistle of straw" or ignores the pacifism of the Sermon on the Mount. But we cannot pretend that the Bible is something we can take or leave as we please. It is a given.

Many centuries have passed now since the church came to understand these as the privileged texts in which we hear God's self-revelation. Having taken the texts as a gift to us, however, we still have to wrestle with them, discover where they make us uncomfortable and find out what kinds of documents they are and the contexts from which they emerge. In particular, we need to ask critical questions of the texts. We can accept the invitation to call God "Father," for there is an important theological point there. At the same time, however, we may also need to find ways of addressing God as "Mother." We have, that is to say, to recognize that the language and structures of the Bible have served to marginalize and exclude women and to render them invisible, and in the same breath we have to refuse to go that way ourselves. If we can do that, then our speech about God will gradually become more thoughtful, and once we can throw aside our linguistic constraints, we shall find ourselves invited to pilgrimage deeper into the mystery of God.

For Christians there is also the central question of who Jesus is. Clearly he is male; he is for that reason also called "Son of God" and "Son of Man." These titles are useful; they say a good deal about Jesus' significance. Nevertheless, we should not use these titles without some thought. We need to be alert to what is going on in them.

In this connection, one set of words that has attracted attention is the lexical field surrounding the words, "King," and its feudal near-relative, "Lord," as well as "kingdom," in phrases like "the kingdom of heaven," which is often on Jesus' lips in the synoptic gospels. Some have produced the imaginative translation "kin-dom" to indicate that Jesus was redefining the old patriarchal family, but my guess is that it is just a little too clever to catch on in ordinary speech, even in ordinary liturgical speech. Some people have adopted the term, "Sovereign" for "King" or "Lord," but African Americans pointed out that they liked using the word "Lord," not in order to indicate the superiority of the male over the female, but because they wanted to assert that God was a higher authority than the old white slave owners who had oppressed them.

For myself, I should find it quite hard to do without the title "Lord." In my own personal devotion it performs an important role, not so much asserting Jesus' power and masculinity, but rather conveying the idea to which Ignatius of Loyola gives expression in his Spiritual Exercises. In the text of the Exercises, Jesus is the companion who shares our uncomfortable life on the overriding mission, the comrade-leader who is prepared to let companionship for the sake of the mission be the primary goal, the one who does not worry about clothing, housing or food. This is an image of Jesus that can animate and inspire me, and the term "Lord" expresses that well for me.

The term also has another advantage that fits smoothly with the Christian experience of God. It enables us to slip, without pausing overlong on the conceptual implications of this move, between speaking of Jesus and speaking of God, in a way that reflects New Testament patterns of speech. Similarly, the New Testament can speak of Jesus as King, and that could sound rather oppressive. But when you see that the place where this happens most prominently is Calvary, where the condemned criminal dies under a sarcastic sign proclaiming him "King of the Jews," it becomes dramatically clear that we are not talking of "king" in the sense that ordinary language or the language of the Roman imperial court gives to it. In other words, the Bible is already geared to making us relativize all speech about God and about Jesus; and that is what I suggest that the feminist critique of the Bible should teach us to do.

Conclusion

To end the chapter, I offer four reflections with regard to our quest for a solution to the crisis over language.

First, any change we make should not be too speedy. It is simply a fact, and not an evasion, that you have to respect people as they are, including their conservatism.

Second, you cannot, on the other hand, ossify the past and proclaim that it was always so and always shall remain so. Words change their meanings, and if we cling to formulations whose meanings change we may be guilty of not being completely faithful to the spirit of the truth. The slogan *extra ecclesiam nulla salus* ("no salvation outside the church"), for example, could not possibly mean the same thing after 1492, when it became known in Europe that there were vast nations of the world that had no way of hearing about Christ or the church, as it had in a world that was coextensive with Christendom. Thus, we cannot today mouth it like a magic talisman. That would be mere superstition.

Third, if change comes slowly, it is not a testimony to people's wickedness, but to the power of religious language. That power is precisely the reason that there is a problem. If the Bible had no power to move, then no one would complain about its view of society, for it would not be influencing anybody. And we must not be naïve about changing it. Suppose that today both the pope and the archbishop of Canterbury were to join with the chief rabbi and the leaders of every Christian church and of every Jewish synagogue and decree that we had to modify our religious and liturgical language. We would not have a new text tomorrow; even if we did, it would be a generation or two before it would be well accepted. Representing God's word to the world is a task that never ends. That however, is not an excuse for not attempting it.

Lastly, it is possible to be too right about things. You probably know the story of the Devil walking with one of his minions and rejoicing when he saw someone pick something up off the ground. The junior devil asked him what the person had picked up, and he replied, "That person has found a piece of the truth." "In that case," asked the neophyte, "why are you so pleased by it?" "Because," said Lucifer, "he will cherish it and concentrate on it alone, and forget about all the rest of the truth."

Feminists have a salutary and painful lesson to teach us, and we must listen attentively. If, however, we were to concentrate only on that part of the truth, we should miss the fullness of God's revelation to us.

CHAPTER THREE

SOME FEMINIST RELIGIOUS THINKERS

QUITE OFTEN IN THIS BOOK I have already used the phrase "many feminist scholars," without doing anything to make more specific the identity of these thinkers. At this point, therefore, I should like to name at least some writers in the field and make some suggestions for further reading, but it is only fair to warn you that what follows will be a skate over fairly thin ice. The thinness is for two reasons: first, to give a proper account of feminist scholarly approaches, even if we restricted ourselves to those who deal only with the New Testament, would take in itself a whole book. Second, feminist biblical scholarship is still only a very young art, and after only thirty years or so it is too early to tell which writers will turn out to be of classical importance. What I propose to do therefore is to mention two names that are of undeniable importance, and then refer to a few other authors, who are very much my own personal choice; and I shall mention only those who can be found in English. The suggestions for further reading at the end of the book are intended to help those who want to delve a little further.

A) MARY DALY

While Mary Daly is not strictly a figure of New Testament scholarship, she cannot be overlooked. Many feminists would regard her as a (some would say *the*) "foremother" of their enterprise. She writes with a humor all her own, and with a crackling anger at the church and at the men who run it.

Much of her most eye-catching work was done in the 1970s and 1980s, and the journey of discovery that she was making during those years may have felt like a far more dramatic ride than it seems several decades later. Nevertheless, the points she is making, sharply conceived and bitingly expressed, are still worth listening to. Of particular importance are her first two books, *The Church and the Second Sex* and *Beyond God the Father*, for in these two she analyzed the nature of patriarchal religion and set forth the problems that feminism has with it. All subsequent writers in the field have built on her work.

Mary Daly is, and has been for many years, a "post-Christian" (this word itself is probably one of her many original coinings). For her, the whole Christian enterprise is irretrievably patriarchal: "the women's critique," she says of the Deutero-Paulines, "is not of a few passages, but a universe of sexist suppositions" (*Beyond God the Father*, p. 5). Her use of English is powerful: phrases like "a transitory euphoria of unhappiness" (p.144) leap from the page, and are effective tools in the hands of this daring and original writer.

The temptation for Christians will be to discount what she says because she is angry or to be fooled into supposing that because she is such a clever writer she has nothing of substance to say. But Daly is a serious scholar with a doctorate in theology and another in philosophy. Her anger is fueled by a sense of having been abominably used and by her judgment that Christianity is intrinsically hostile both to women and to the "Elemental Philosophy" (see her book *Pure Lust*) that in her view it displaced, and which she would restore.

Some of her writing, such as the characteristically titled *Gyn/Ecology*, is not precisely pleasant, but then it is not meant to be. Mary Daly speaks for many women who have passed through and beyond Christianity, especially perhaps Catholic Christianity, because they feel it has nothing more to say to them, indeed has already said far too much of the wrong sort of thing. She quotes, early in her "New Feminist Post-Christian Introduction" to *The Church and the Second Sex*, her own remark to a journalist who asked a somewhat rash question about equality for women in the church: "Why, I wondered, would anyone want 'equality' in the church?...A woman's asking for equality in the church would be comparable to a black person's demanding equality in the Ku Klux Klan" (p. 6).

It is her view that all religion is hostile to women, for it represents "a planetary caste system whose very existence has been made invisible to us" (p.132). She is deceptively easy to read, which makes some of her critics inclined to parody her rather than engage in real dialogue. But it is important to notice her efforts to "rethink the familiar." Christians have not won a victory if we dismiss post-Christians as "not worth talking to"; we have merely postponed a reckoning. The people for whom Mary Daly speaks have something to say that we ought to hear, however uncomfortable it may be to listen.

B) Elisabeth Schüssler Fiorenza

Like Mary Daly, Elisabeth Schüssler Fiorenza is from a Catholic background, and though she is thoroughly critical of many aspects of the Catholic tradition, would not consider herself post-Christian. A professor at Harvard Divinity School, Schüssler Fiorenza is a towering figure as biblical scholar and historian of the early church. It is not merely that she can hold her own in what she calls "malestream" scholarship; her concern is to rewrite the agenda and point to the questions that mainstream (elite, white, male, patriarchal) scholarship has failed to ask. Her strength is in the area of hermeneutics, the branch of thought that examines how we can mean or communicate anything at all, and that probes the philosophical underpinnings of our attempts to do a deceptively simple thing like reading the Bible.

At the heart of her enterprise is her perception that "all discourses represent political interests" (*But She Said,* p. 3), which means that even biblical texts are written from a particular point of view and with the interest of a particular group in mind. There is, that is to say, no such thing as "value-free" or "objective" discovery of the original meaning of the texts, but only, as we have already seen, the act of reading through a particular "lens." Given this insight, the reader must, in her view, "deconstruct the dominant paradigms of biblical interpretation" so as to see the texts afresh. The place where this is to be done is what Schüssler Fiorenza calls the *ekklesia gunaikon,* or "women-church." This is an important notion, for one of the key elements in all feminist scholarship is the priority it gives to the act of sharing women's experiences.

One of her great strengths lies in her ability to distinguish different ways of approaching biblical texts (and nonbiblical works also, for she casts her net very wide over the world of the first century), and to make explicit the ways in which they are different and the ways in which they further or hinder the aim of transforming the world. As we have indicated in previous chapters, feminist biblical scholarship, and perhaps all feminist work, has to do with the struggle for the dignity and equality of all human beings. Schüssler Fiorenza takes a particular interest in the task of "making women visible" in texts and stories where their voices have been absent or lost.

Schüssler Fiorenza has written a great deal, and to single out the works that *must* be read is a delicate enterprise. But there are a few of her works that we cannot afford to neglect. *But She Said*–the title comes from the Canaanite woman's response to Jesus at Matthew 15:27–tries to look at how women can interject their "but," their particular perspective, into the standard way of reading these passages so as to enable a different, and liberating, understanding of the text. *In Memory of Her* is an attempt to reconstruct the beginnings of Christianity from a critical feminist point of view, asserting that the women, as well as the men, were there and actively helped to shape the history of Christianity right from the start. The title is taken, with conscious irony, from Mark 14:9.

Another significant book is *Jesus, Miriam's Child, Sophia's Prophet*, which attempts to uncover the presuppositions of feminist Christology. Some readers may start a bit at the idea of a *feminist* approach to the question of who Jesus is, but they may care to reflect that kyriarchy (a word coined by Elisabeth Schüssler Fiorenza) is everywhere. This is especially the case when theology attempts to unpack the significance for all humanity of one who was unambiguously male.

Lastly, mention should be made of *Searching the Scriptures*, a two-volume introduction offering various insights into feminist theory and commentary on the New Testament and other Jewish and early Christian writings. Schüssler Fiorenza served as the editor and wrote only the two introductions. I mention the book at this stage, partly because it underlines her contribution to feminist biblical scholarship, not merely writing but also encouraging others to write, and also because readers may find it helpful to know of a feminist commentary on Scripture texts when we start to read them in the next few chapters.

c) LUISE SCHOTTROFF

Luise Schottroff is professor of New Testament at the University of Kassel in Germany. Her main work, entitled *Lydia's Impatient Sisters,* looks at the women who joined the Christian movement in its infant years. The book is a social history of the ordinary life of the women who attached themselves to the movement, making careful and respectful use of the evidence so as to let the reader see what it was like. This is, it must be said, a different way of doing biblical scholarship, and it has led her into career-threatening trouble.

It is a stimulating and provocative book full of helpful insights into feminist method and its application to the biblical texts. One reservation some have voiced about her approach, and it applies to a number of other feminist writers, is its assumption that the liberation of women is inextricably interwoven with the liberalization of laws concerning abortion and homosexuality.

d) ROSEMARY RADFORD RUETHER

Rosemary Radford Ruether's book *Sexism and God-Talk* is an enormously wide-ranging work because of her insight that feminism touches the whole of life. She has set the agenda for many Catholic feminists in recent years. A good way to grasp what she is trying to do would be to read the "Feminist Midrash on the Gospel in Three Acts," with which *Sexism and God-Talk* begins. It is symptomatic of her wide range—and methodologically of great importance to what she is about—that she employs "all usable traditions" (p. 21). This means she uses not just Scripture, but also ancient Christian traditions that lie outside of the Bible, what we know as *apocrypha.* She draws on not just mainstream theological themes, but also those that surface elsewhere in ancient religion and philosophy. In addition, Ruether makes use of post-Christian worldviews such as Marxism, liberalism and romanticism.

It is Rosemary Radford Ruether who coined the neologism "God/ess," to which we referred in an earlier chapter. Her aim is expressed in these characteristically robust and uncompromising statements:

> ...an encounter with our authentic selves resurrected from underneath the alienated self. It is not experienced against, but in and through relationships, healing our broken relations with our bodies, with other people, with nature. We have no adequate name for the true God/ess, the "I am who I shall become." Intimations of Her/His name will appear as we emerge from false naming of God/ess modeled on patriarchal alienation." (p. 71)

E) ELIZABETH JOHNSON

Elizabeth Johnson, too, belongs solidly within the Catholic Christian tradition and, like all good theologians, is looking for new ways of talking about God—what she describes in her book *She Who Is* as "fresh language about the mystery of God" (p. 21). She seeks to counter what seems to be the message of much mainstream Christian theology, that "God is male, or at least more like a man than a woman, or at least more fittingly addressed as male than as female" (p. 5). The title, *She Who Is,* is also a title for God, "a divine title signifying the creative, relational power of being who enlivens, suffers with, sustains, and enfolds the universe" (p.13). As is the case with almost all feminist theologians, she lays great stress on women's experience and on the importance of language.

Johnson looks at an issue that gives many Christians pause, on both the feminist and the more traditionalist wings, namely, the maleness of Jesus, and she offers a rigorous and stimulating treatment of feminist Christology. Her book also includes an examination of the doctrine of the Trinity. In a beautiful exposition of that doctrine, she speaks of it as expressing "a livingness in God, a dynamic coming and going with the world that points to an inner divine circling around in unimaginable relation" (p. 192). Part IV of this book, attractively and suggestively entitled "Dense Symbols and Their Dark Light," is of immense importance in this enterprise.

While there is not space here for as full a treatment as she deserves, these words, taken from the epilogue of the book, give us a sense of what she is trying to do: "No language about God will ever be fully adequate to the burning mystery which it signifies. But a more inclusive way of speaking can come about that bears the ancient wisdom with a new justice" (p. 273). We can apply these words to all the issues that feminism raises for Christianity.

F) MARGARET HEBBLETHWAITE

Margaret Hebblethwaite is different from the foregoing writers in that she is a theologian and journalist with a background in Ignatian spirituality. In her work entitled *Six New Gospels,* she gives six different views of Jesus, placing them on the lips of six women who, according to the gospels, knew him in various ways. She is explicitly not aiming at historical reconstruction, as our three previous authors were, but at rediscovering "the suppressed role of women" because "the evangelists intended to write a male-dominated story." Like Elisabeth Schüssler Fiorenza, she employs historical imagination to fill the gaps. The result is a touching and beautiful series of sketches that, when taken together, present a challenge to the customary view about the role of women in the Bible. The stories are easy to read, and the reader can return to them over and again, each time discovering a further depth and richness. In common with other feminist approaches, Hebblethwaite's method takes as its primary focus not so much the text of the New Testament, but the experience of women and the way Jesus can speak to that experience.

G) KWOK PUI-LAN

All of the authors we have mentioned so far are women of the West; but one of the developments in feminism has been the contribution, which has often been spirited and questioning, of women from cultures other than the dominant one. The experience of women in non-"mainstream" cultures has given rise to new and different questions about the place of women.

Kwok Pui-Lan is an Asian feminist who offers questions that have still to be tackled. The easiest way of introducing her might be by way of an extensive quotation from the introduction to her book *Discovering the Bible in the Non-Biblical World:*

> I come to you as a Chinese, deeply moved by recent happenings in China [these words were written in 1989] and impressed by the thousands of Chinese students who have given up their lives for democracy. I come to you as a woman, mother of an eight-year-old daughter, who has listened to Asian women's stories, shared their pain, and rejoiced in their hope. I come to you as a Christian theologian, having received years of theological training yet refusing to follow the western male type of doing theology." (p. ix)

One notices a different tone that makes clear that the feminist approach is *different*. First, the author is explicitly politically aware, a characteristic that marks out feminist from "patriarchal" biblical scholarship. For feminists, "the personal is always political." Second, she is alive to the importance of relationships and of ethnicity: the fact that she has a daughter of a particular age makes a difference to the kind of theology that she does, as does her awareness of being Chinese. Third, as with much feminist writing, there is the weight placed on experience, and in particular the experience of those who suffer. Fourth, and this is very important, she is conscious of being *different:* she is different from white males and different, too, from white feminists. Lastly, she is on the side of the down-trodden and the oppressed, especially those who are women.

In all of this she is seeking a distinctively Asian style of doing theology, just as feminists from other backgrounds—African, African American, Jewish, Hispanic—want to hammer out their own ways of being theologians and exegetes, through first listening to the stories of women in their own cultures and then reflecting on them. Like all feminist scholars, Kwok Pui-Lan points to questions of authority and power, and she takes a characteristic view on the canon of Scripture: "the formation of a religious canon is clearly a matter of power." Her distinctive contribution is to join other representatives of marginalized cultures in pointing to situations such as those of the Native Americans, of tribal peoples in Taiwan, of Maoris in New Zealand and of Christians in Palestine, where the Book of Exodus, so beloved of Latin American and other liberation theologians, is not experienced as proclaiming a God of freedom because of the treatment accorded in its pages to the indigenous cultures.

H) MERCY AMBA ODUYOYE

Mercy Amba Oduyoye, a Nigerian theologian belonging to the Methodist tradition, speaks for many African women, from whom, I suspect, we still have a great deal to hear. In a poem that she places at the very beginning of *Daughters of Anowa,* she says, in the name of all those women in Africa and beyond who are thrust to the margins, "I do not speak much, but I am not without a voice" (p. vii). She is very alive to the issues of both gender and race. Underlying all of her writing is the question, "What is woman?" and the answer, "Women are human." To those who would argue that this is hardly an earth-shattering truth, she points to the situation of women in African society and contests the slogan uttered by some African males "our women are not oppressed" by dryly commenting that "a certain hermeneutic of suspicion is required whenever an African male proclaims that the African female is powerful" (p.114). But like many feminists she has to argue in two directions at once, for she will not allow the racist assumption of some in the West that all African males are patriarchs, and yet she indicates how complex African culture is in this respect. She also makes the point that Africans are "incurably religious" and shows how African goddesses succeeded in crossing the Atlantic and surfacing in places like Brazil and Haiti in Christian disguises. At this point Oduyoye joins hands with *mujerista* (Latin American feminist) theologians.

She is critical of African Independent churches, arguing that the traditional African views of male superiority and male privilege have been reinforced by both traditional religious biases and the Western churches' exclusion from ministry. And she is equally critical of the mainline Christian churches but argues that both these groups may draw help from African culture, for "the African mind contains an image of a motherly Father or a fatherly Mother as the Source of Being" (p. 179). At the heart of her argument is the simple insight that "God cannot be said to have brought into being one variety of humanity that is inherently not up to the mark. Our cardinal human sin has always been that of broken relations with the source of our being, God. The result has been brokenness in human relations and in our relation with the rest of creation." This idea puts her within the mainstream of Christian feminist thought, as does her firmly held view that "whatever is keeping the subordination of women alive in the Church cannot be the Spirit of God" (p.182). Patriarchal structures, she argues, conceal the beauty and connectedness with the divine which Jesus' naming of God as Father should give us. And she speaks for all feminists and all serious theologians when she proclaims "we must refuse to cooperate in the devaluation of our persons or humanity" (p. 202).

I) Lavinia Byrne

Our final author in this brief overview of the field in English is Lavinia Byrne, a religious sister of the Institute of the Blessed Virgin Mary. Her book, *Women at the Altar: The Ordination of Women in The Catholic Church,* is interesting not least from the point of view of method. Her aim is to make the case for the ordination of women in the Catholic Church. Unlike our other authors, she starts not with the experience of women, but with what the Catholic Church teaches about women and how that teaching has in fact raised feminist consciousness in the church. She argues that "feminism is a product of Christianity" (p. 57), doubtless to the surprise of people on both left and right. Only then does she consider the contribution of feminist writings and how we are to achieve Christian community in our present age. Finally, she examines ways of establishing ethical principles for the whole of humanity and methods for establishing appropriate models of leadership.

In common with many feminists, she emphasizes the importance of sharing and storytelling as part of the method. Byrne gives a high priority to human experience and a correspondingly lower emphasis on "getting it right." Like many feminist thinkers who still retain their allegiance to the mainline churches, she finds herself talking in two directions: "Secular feminism trashes the Churches for what they have offered women; most Christians are terrified of secular feminists. And standing in the firing line are those women theologians who are brave enough to try to keep an open conversation with both sides" (p. 74). This is something that we shall do well to remember: Christian feminists can distill a wisdom that will enable us to hear what the feminists are saying, and it may also enable us to see that the churches, even those that have been so reluctant to listen to women's voices, have light of their own to shed on the darkened path that lies ahead of us.

Conclusion

In light of this brief glance at the "spectrum" of feminist opinion, it becomes clear that it is not possible to neatly categorize feminist thought from left to right, from ultraviolet to infrared. Things have not yet sufficiently settled down in the field. To force the different feminists, who have far more in common than the things that divide them, into neat and separate categories will seriously misrepresent the situation. Nevertheless, a challenge faces them as they struggle to find their voices and make those voices audible to the rest of us, to be "their own voice" and at the same time "a feminist voice," and then to speak to the whole human race of the lessons they have learned on our behalf, whether they are Jewish feminists such as Judith Plaskow or Amy-Jill Levine, or whether they are African, womanist or *Mujeristas* (Latin American feminists). One of the great gifts of feminists to us is their endeavor to make audible the voices of other women, of whatever race or class and regardless of "academic status." The trick is to maintain the different kinds of feminism without "balkanization," to work together in the service of humanity as a whole. Feminist scholars, with their emphasis on experience and "real life," and their call for the transformation of unjust structures, may well enable us to discover theology and the Bible as "relevant" and transforming.

Part II

In the second part of the book, we shall be looking at some of the texts of the New Testament that are relevant to our quest. We shall not be looking at all of them, for the resulting book would be far too long; and we shall approach them by way of running commentary rather than in-depth analysis. The aim will be to hint at how one might pray or preach these passages with sensitivity to women by way of translations of the texts and a brief comment. The translations and commentaries belong very closely together and are intended to invite the reader to a deeper acquaintance with the scriptural texts. It may be helpful to have your Bible open before you as you read these pages.

In looking at these texts I shall try to answer the double question: "Where and how are the women?" But you could equally well ask yourself: Can I pray these texts? Or, if your stance is a little more detached (and if you are a male), you might wonder: If I were a woman, what would I find difficult or repellent about the passage? I shall generally be giving an optimistic reading of the texts, making the assumption that they can be a life-giving word to women as well as men. For reasons of space I shall not attempt to consider in detail every single New Testament text. This approach has a weakness, of course: some would say that my failure to analyze every single text means that I do not give sufficient weight to the "inscribed patriarchy" of the whole New Testament, while others might argue that the imbalance of my presentation is unfair to the New Testament as a whole.

It seems appropriate to turn first to the gospels, which are not, either in the intention of their authors or in fact, "lives of Jesus" in the same sense as modern biographies. Instead, they are different yet similar compilations of stories and sayings that had been retold by Christians for at least a generation after Jesus' death before they were finally written down. Nevertheless, they can still tell us quite a lot. There can be no doubt at all that there was a person called Jesus who came from Nazareth in Galilee, and that he was a remarkable person who taught and preached and healed people. It is certain that he died by crucifixion under Pontius Pilate, and that two days later his followers came to the conclusion that he was alive, a conclusion to which many millions still assent. Furthermore, for the purposes of our inquiry, we can say with a degree of confidence that he had a gift for dealing with people, and that there is no sign at all in the stories told about him that he shared the view, common enough in the ancient world, that women were inferior to men. In fact, the stories told of him suggest that he was at ease with women, and dealt with them as persons, not as threats. And despite recent speculation, he was not married.

In the next four chapters, however, we shall be looking not at Jesus alone, but also at those who told the Jesus stories, to see if we can detect their attitudes toward women. So we shall look at some texts from each of the four evangelists. We do not know, of course, who these four evangelists were. Each gospel is given a name, but that does not mean that they were written by, respectively, a tax collector, Peter's secretary, Paul's doctor and traveling companion, and one of the sons of Zebedee. The names, Matthew, Mark, Luke and John, represent the guesswork of a later generation, and all that we know of the authors is what their texts reveal of them. Probably they were men, although a case might be made for Mark's gospel being written by a woman.

Each of these authors has his (or her) own angle on the events being narrated; that stance is not necessarily the stance of Jesus, even though in each case Jesus is the hero. They see Jesus, that is to say, through their own "lens." The task, then, is to discover what that "lens" was and then to get back to Jesus' "lens"—to establish what view they and Jesus held of women. It is perfectly acceptable therefore for us to say, "This is the way that Luke saw it - this is not the way I see it." Christians who are anxious to read and pray the gospels need to distinguish the issues and questions that they bring to the text from the issues and questions that are already present in the text. Therefore, it does not mean that there has been some kind of mistake if a faithful Christian finds that the attitude toward women expressed in this or that gospel is not one that he or she shares. It is still possible for you to pray your way through them, keeping in mind that your agenda may be rather different from that of each evangelist.

CHAPTER FOUR

MARK'S GOSPEL—WOMEN AS MODEL DISCIPLES

WE START WITH MARK'S GOSPEL because it was most probably the earliest of the four to be written, and both Matthew and Luke almost certainly knew Mark. This gospel seeks to answer two questions: first, Who is this Jesus? and second, If Jesus is like this, then what should his disciples be like? The first question is obviously the central one, but since we are dealing with a gospel (indeed with the creator of the literary form) intended to be read by disciples and would-be disciples, the second question is always there just below the surface. The question "Who is Jesus?" is not an easy one, as the disciples reveal by their stumbling bemusement, and runs as a theme throughout Mark's gospel. It is true that in the first verse Jesus is described as "Messiah, Son of God," but we do not really discover what that means until the mysterious ending, when a Roman centurion who watches Jesus die, alone and abandoned apparently even by God, says (15:39), "...in sober truth, this fellow was Son of God." Therefore, and connectedly, we do not really succeed in answering the question about what Jesus' disciples are like until we come to the gospel's original ending: "...and [the women] said nothing to anybody; for they were afraid." But that is to anticipate.

In the process of establishing who Jesus is, the evangelist throws up at us a number of questions, some of which are answered in the text, while others are left unanswered, leaving the reader to "fill in the blanks." So, in 1:27 the crowds who see Jesus casting out an unclean spirit ask, "What is this?" and provide a sort of answer (or perhaps just a statement of their deeper puzzlement), "...a new teaching, with authority." In the next chapter it is some scribes who ask a question. When Jesus says, "...your sins are forgiven," we hear them ask, "Why does this man speak in this way? He is blaspheming! Who can forgive sins except One, namely God?" (2:7). This question is not directly answered, but before their eyes the man is healed and carries away his bed. The thoughtful reader is thus encouraged to answer the question for himself or herself.

Something similar takes place at the end of chapter 4, when Jesus, who had been fast asleep in the prow of the boat, is awakened, and tells the wind and sea, "Be quiet! No more noise!" This leaves the unidentified "them" muttering to each other, "Who is this, then, that both the wind and the sea obey him?" (4:41). No answer is given to the question. Once again, the reader must "fill in the blanks." In chapter 6 the question is posed twice, both times in an aggressive or unsympathetic way. In Jesus' home town, when he preaches in the synagogue,

> ...many heard and were amazed, saying, "Where did this fellow get these things from? And what is this wisdom that has been given to him, and the powers of this sort that have happened through his hands? Is not this fellow the carpenter, the son of Mary and the brother of Jacob and Joses and Judah and Simon? And aren't his sisters here with us?" (6:2–3).

Once again, the question goes unanswered, and the reader is invited to decide whether the description here offered of Jesus is adequate in terms of the gospel.

Later in that same chapter the question of Jesus' identity is raised again, this time by Herod and his cronies:

> ...they said that John the Baptist had risen from the dead, and that's why these powers were at work in him. But others said that it was Elijah, and others again said "a prophet, like one of the prophets"; but when Herod heard about it, he said, "The one I decapitated, John, that fellow is risen." (6: 14)

Once more, the reader is invited to examine these possible categories for Jesus and to answer the implied question.

Those same attempts at describing Jesus appear again at 8:28–29:

John the Baptist, Elijah, one of the prophets. But the disciples are for the first time directly invited to answer the question, "And who do *you* say that I am?" Peter speaks for them all and affirms, "You are the Messiah." Notice what happens next, however: first, Jesus explains what kind of a Messiah he really is (31–32); then Peter resists that interpretation, finding it altogether too strong, and is rebuked in the most dramatic possible terms (33); and, finally, the moral is drawn concerning our second question, "What must Jesus' disciples therefore be like?" (34–38).

Twice more in the gospel the question of the identity of Jesus is raised and not answered, except, between the lines, by the reader: in chapter 10 the rich man dashes up to Jesus and asks a question about inheriting eternal life, addressing him for the purpose as "good master." Jesus' answer is discouraging, concentrating instead on an apparent irrelevance, "Why do you call me good? No one is good, except One, God" (10:18). This forces the reader to ask whether or not this is an appropriate form of address for Jesus. Then, after Jesus' prophetic gesture in the Temple he is asked:

> By what authority do you do these things? Or who gave you this authority to do these things? (11:28).

The question is not really answered, or is adroitly side-stepped by Jesus, and the reader must face the question of whether Jesus really is authorized to do these things and, if so, how one should respond to him.

Finally, in the fourteenth chapter, the question of Jesus' identity is asked again and (when it no longer matters, after a period of silence on Jesus' part) dramatically answered:

> Again the High Priest asked him and said to him, "Are you the Messiah, the Son of the Blessed One?" And Jesus said, "I am. And you will see the Son of Man sitting on the right hand of power and going with the clouds of heaven." (14:61–6)

This is taken to be a blasphemous self-identification on Jesus' part, and once more the reader has to decide what he is saying and whether he is correct, and to "fill in the blanks" accordingly.

We have already mentioned the centurion's verdict at Jesus' death, but it might be good to remind ourselves of it. The cross itself asks a question: "Who is this criminal, alone and abandoned as he apparently is, who dies railing at God *'Elohi, Eelhi, lema Sabachthani?'*" (15:34). The unlikely observer answers, "It was the Son of God" (15:39), to which the reader might respond, first, "Well, is that so?" and second, "Well, in that case, what should I do; how should I behave?" We have already seen the answers to these two questions at the end of chapter 8 of the gospel, where Peter's correct identification of Jesus as Messiah led to instruction about what Jesus' disciples should look like: denying themselves, taking up the cross, surrendering their lives, not being ashamed of the Son of Man.

A less immediately obvious answer might be: watch the women. That is why we have made such a long and courtly advance to the question of the women in the second gospel. My suggestion is that the women in this gospel are the exemplary disciples, the ones who alone get it right (with, as we shall see, one dramatic exception).

As in all the remaining chapters of this book, I shall here present you with unfamiliar translations of familiar passages. This means that there will be some apparent repetitions, but that need not matter, for we are trying to grasp each gospel as an individual document, and to see in it where and how are the women.

Two points of awkwardness I experience in translating Mark can usefully be mentioned here. Firstly, he often uses a historic present, as in the English colloquialism, "then she says to me...", referring to a conversation in the past. You will find that very often I have preserved this in order to protect the Marcan flavor, but occasionally I have put it into the past tense. A second peculiarity of Mark's style is a flurry of unreferred pronouns—"he told him," for example, when it is not clear in a dialogue who is doing what and to whom. Generally, I have left them as in the original except where a change was absolutely necessary in order to clarify what is going on, and then only when it was quite evident in Mark's text who was being referred to.

A) SIMON'S MOTHER-IN-LAW (1:29–31)

The first encounter with a woman in the gospel is described in these terms:

> And immediately coming out of the synagogue they came to the house of Simon and Andrew with Jacob and Johanan. Now Simon's mother-in-law was lying down with a fever, and straightaway they tell him about her. And he came forward and raised her up, taking her by the hand. And the fever left her. And she deaconed for him.

Since this is the first encounter in the first gospel to be written, it inevitably sets the tone for our understanding of Jesus' dealings with women. We may presume that the mother-in-law was lying in the women's quarters, off-limits to men. Jesus, however, as soon as he was told of her affliction, took not the slightest notice of these boundaries. Nor did he bother with questions of possible defilement, because he actually took her by the hand. He cures her effortlessly; but then comes the significant moment, which I have belabored a shade clumsily by translating the verb as "she deaconed." It is the word for ministry and service, which became, as it still is today, a technical term for a church hierarch. More than that, it is used on a few key occasions in Mark's gospel: there are the angels who "minister to Jesus" after his sojourn in the desert (1:13); then the verb is used of Jesus himself ("not to be served, but to serve") at 10:45, with the related noun a little earlier ("whoever wants to become great among you shall be your *diakonos,*" 10:43). And there is another passage that we shall come to at the end. For the moment, let us notice that these words describe a characteristic that we may properly expect in a disciple of Jesus, and the first to show this quality is a woman.

B) JESUS' FAMILY PROBLEMS (3:21, 31–35)

Our second passage is really two passages, which "sandwich" some dark allegations about Jesus being in league with Beelzeboul:

And his people when they heard, they came out to arrest him. For they said that he was crazy....

And his mother comes, and his brothers, and standing outside they sent to him, summoning [or: "inviting"] him. And a crowd sat around him, and they said to him, "Look, your mother and your brothers ["and your sisters," according to some good manuscripts] are outside looking for you. And he answered them, "Who is my mother and my brothers?" And looking around at those who sat around him in a circle, he says, "Look, *here* are my mother and my brothers. For whoever does the will of God, that person is my brother and sister and mother."

According to Mark 3:20, the reason why "Jesus' people" or "those near Jesus" wanted to arrest him was that he was not setting aside enough time for them to eat. Now we might feel that it is rather creditable to be so busy about God's work that meals cannot be fitted in. In that culture, however, to behave in this "over the top" fashion brought shame on the family (if indeed it is his family making the fuss here). After those deeply unpleasant accusations of devilworship, they make another attempt, and it is now certainly the family that is in question.

Jesus' response can sound a little harsh, but he is not so much rejecting his mother or his brothers as redefining the nature of family. Jesus' family now becomes those who do God's will, and that includes both men and women. Insofar as this passage deals with women as such, it may therefore be said to tend in the direction of equality. We should recall here the passages at 6:1–6, where those from his hometown are scandalized by Jesus, because of the shock caused by someone whose identity and family were so well known to them who showed such wisdom and healing powers. What the reader of the gospel is here being invited to do is not merely reflect on the question "Who is this Jesus?", but to take a particularly exalted option about the answer to that question and not merely come to Mark's answer about Jesus' identity—to sit round Jesus in a circle and with him find out what the will of God is and then do it.

C) THE HEALING OF TWO WOMEN (5:21–43)

Our next text is again two texts, sandwiching each other, and therefore to be interpreted closely together. They follow the story of the Gerasene demoniac (5:1–20), in which Jesus shows a similar disregard of the possibilities of defilement. Immediately after this, Jesus gets back in his boat:

> And when Jesus crossed over in the boat, back to the other side, a great crowd gathered to him; and he was by the sea. And one of the synagogue rulers comes, Jairus by name, and when he saw him he fell at his feet, and earnestly asked him, many times over, saying, "My little daughter is at the point of death; [I beg] you to come and lay hands on her, so that she may be saved, and may live." And he went off with him; and a great crowd followed him, and they pressed around him.
>
> And there was a woman who had had a flow of blood for twelve years, and who had suffered a good deal from many doctors, had spent all that she had by her, and was in no way helped but rather got worse. She had heard about Jesus, and she came up behind him in the crowd, and, from behind, touched his clothing. For she said, "If I can just touch his clothes, I'll be saved." And immediately the fountain of her blood dried up, and she knew in her body that she was healed of the scourge. And immediately, Jesus, knowing in himself that power had gone out of him, turned round in the crowd and said, "Who touched my clothing?" And his disciples said to him, "You see the crowd pressing around you, and you say, 'Who touched me?'" And Jesus kept on looking round to see the woman who had done this. And the woman, afraid and trembling, knowing what had happened to her, came and fell before him, and told him the whole truth. But he said to her, "Daughter, your faith has saved you. Go in peace, and be clean of your scourge."
>
> While he was still speaking, people came from the synagogue ruler's house, saying, "Your daughter has died; why do you still trouble the teacher?" But Jesus overheard the remark being made, and said to the synagogue ruler, "Don't be afraid; just believe." And he allowed no one to follow on with him, except for Peter and Jacob and Johanan the brother of Jacob. And they come to the

house of the synagogue ruler, and he sees the clamor and them weeping and wailing prolifically, and he went in and said to them, "Why are you clamoring and weeping? The little child is not dead, but asleep." And they laughed him down; but he threw them all out, and took the father of the child and her mother, and the ones who were with him, and goes into where the little child was. And taking the hand of the little child, he says to her, "Talitha koum," which is translated, "Little girl, I tell you, arise." And straightaway, the little girl rose up and walked about. For she was twelve years old. And they were amazed with a great amazement; and he gave them several instructions that nobody should know of this. And he said that she should be given something to eat.

This is a long passage, but worth looking at, since Mark has put together two stories about women for us, presumably to read the one in the light of the other. We cannot comment on every aspect of the passage but can at least point to one or two elements of it.

In the first story, we discover that the little girl, daughter of a named synagogue ruler (and therefore perhaps moving in a slightly unexpected circle) is on the point of death. She is therefore in double danger of creating defilement, for she is about to become a corpse, and, as we discover at the end, she is at the age when she might be expected to menstruate. Then, like the other woman, what is asked for is that she be "saved," which, in my view, is a notch or two above being merely "restored to life." Note the great crowd, pressing round, and "following." This last word tends to be a term indicating discipleship in Mark, but at this stage it needs to be taken with a grain of salt. Discipleship in this gospel is only for the few who are prepared to accept the cost, not for large and exuberant crowds. In any case, the throng is part of the artistic setting for the second story in the pair, which now begins.

This second story is one of the loveliest stories in the gospel, and quite remarkable for the fact that, except for verses 30–32, it is told entirely through the eyes of the woman. Notice how it stresses the length of her suffering: twelve years, the same as the time for which the little girl had been alive. To have a disorder of this (presumably) gynecological sort is an almost unimaginable alienation; we should think of it in terms of that amount of solitary confinement or incarceration in a lunatic asylum. Nor had the doctors been of much use. Like the widow whom we shall meet later, she had spent everything she had in order to put an end to what Mark accurately and imaginatively describes as a "scourge" (the word means "whip" or, by extension, "chastisement"). Now she takes the initiative for herself, and Mark describes her as touching the hem of Jesus' garment "from behind." This surreptitiousness is partly because in her desperation she is deliberately subjecting Jesus to ritual impurity, and thus she needs to do it unobserved, but Mark may also mean us to understand that she is behaving as a disciple would, "coming behind, or after," Jesus.

Next, Mark allows us to overhear what she is planning to do, and we learn that what she wanted was exactly what Jairus had asked on behalf of his daughter, namely, to be "saved." That implies more than being healed. It involves a restoration of her relationships—with other people, with God, and with herself—all of which will have been interrupted by her dreadful disease. For the moment, however, she must settle for second best, because as she touches Jesus' cloak, she is instantaneously and effortlessly healed. This is something that she knows "in her body."

Jesus also knows it, but at a different cognitive level, "in himself." He not only knows it, he knows that the power has gone out of him. Contrast the knowledge of the woman and Jesus' knowledge, however, with the jeering ignorance of the disciples ("Do you see the crowd pressing around you?..."). Jesus and the woman alone understand what has happened, and so Jesus pays no attention to the disciples' response, but continues to look around. And here is another thing that the translations often gloss over, but which is absolutely clear in the Greek: Jesus knows that it is a *woman* he is looking for.

He does not have to spend long in his search, however, for she comes forward, and we have the sense of Jesus and the woman sharing a private world to which the disciples are as yet too insensitive to gain access. She comes forward "in fear and trembling" because she knows what Jesus knows and what nobody else in the crowd has begun to realize—that she has been in touch with the divine. Now the process is completed, and this in two ways. First, she is addressed as "daughter," which brings her into a family that she did not have before. Second, having hitherto been merely healed, she is pronounced "saved," which is what we know (since we were allowed to overhear her thoughts) she was looking for. It is a remarkable vignette of two people who understand each other, surrounded by the uncomprehending, and Mark has depicted it with an artistry that should surprise those who are misled by his slightly casual Greek into supposing him an indifferent writer.

Her story is now closed, but it is very much in our minds as we continue the journey to the house where Jairus's child is sick, and we wonder what Jesus might do for her. The first thing that happens is that some people from Jairus's house bring bad news in a manner that must have seemed unsympathetic even in that society, where death was more accepted as a part of life than it is in contemporary Western society: "Your daughter is dead; why do you still trouble the teacher?" In response to this insensitivity, Jesus teaches a double lesson. First, although he is a teacher, he is not one of those whom you have to be careful of not troubling. Second, he indicates that Jairus and he understand each other, for he instructs him, "Don't be afraid; just believe." Both of these verbs are appropriate for what happens in an encounter with God. No one else is allowed to "follow on with" him (an awkward phrase trying to translate a difficult Greek idea that has at least something to do with discipleship), except the girl's family and the "inner cabinet" of Jesus' disciples. Notice women are not entirely absent from the group; the little girl's mother is there.

The healing follows, and, once again, it is effortless. As before, it involves touching and Jesus' complete indifference to ritual pollution—neither the touch of a corpse nor contact with a menstruating woman causes him the smallest bother. Instead, in a charming way that indicates how Jesus saw people as human beings and not as categories, the story ends with him giving instructions for this twelve-year-old to be fed.

D) Two Women Who Are Not to Be Imitated (6:17–29)

Next we encounter two rather different women, the only ones who get things wrong in the gospel of Mark. The two first verses of the story concern the question, "Who is Jesus?", the first of the two questions which, I have argued, the gospel seeks to answer. The rest of the story might serve as a kind of answer to the second question, "What should Jesus' disciples be like?", only from the opposite end: this is how disciples do *not* behave:

> For Herod had sent and arrested John, and locked him in prison, on account of Herodias the wife of his brother Philip, because he had married her. For John was telling Herod, "It is not permissible for you to have your brother's wife." And Herodias had it in for him, and wanted to kill him; but she was unable to, because Herod stood in awe of John; he knew him for a virtuous and holy man, and he kept him alive. And when he listened to him, he was a good deal puzzled, and he enjoyed listening to him.
>
> And there came a "window of opportunity" when Herod, on the occasion of his birthday, gave a meal, for the VIPs and the commanding officers, and for the most prominent people in Galilee. And his daughter Herodias came in and danced. And she pleased Herod and those who were dining with him. The King said to the girl, "Ask of me anything you want, and I shall give it to you." And he promised her many times over, "Whatever you ask me, I shall give you, up to and including half my kingdom." She went out and said to her mother, "What shall I ask for?" She said, "The head of John the Baptist." And straightaway she went eagerly back in to the King, and made her request: "I want you to give me the head of John the Baptist, on a dish, right now."
>
> And the King was very sad; because of his promises, and because of those who were at the party, he was reluctant to welsh on her. And there and then the King sent a trooper to bring his head. He went off and decapitated him in the prison, and brought his head on a dish. And he gave it to the little girl; and the little girl gave it to her mother. And his disciples came and took his corpse, and placed it in a tomb.

It is a dreadfully sad story, and as Mark tells it, part of a battle between husband and wife. He gives us a glimpse of Herod's head-scratching delight in hearing John talk and a less attractive insight into Herodias's determination to have no more prophetic denunciations of her marital state. Certainly we are not intended to see this lady as a docile or submissive wife. We cannot help observing the foolishness of Herod's bragging promise, reminiscent of that awful story of Jephtah, at which readers get so justifiably indignant (Judges 11:30–40). In response, the enormously powerful Herodias makes the terrible request of John's head. One should notice that the dancing daughter, also called Herodias, rather confusingly, is quite excited about the idea; and not only that, but she also adds some embroidery of her own by asking for the head to come on a dish, which starkly underlines the grotesque horror of the gift that is being given. So Herod is trapped, and lacks the integrity to lose face; therefore he gives the order, which is obeyed to the letter.

The clue to the story is in the beginning and the end. For it starts, as we have seen, with the first of our questions, "Who is Jesus?" and it ends with disciples, not those of Jesus, but John's, coming to collect the body. The story puts the question quite bluntly: which side would you rather be on? All those present at the dinner party were guilty in some way or other. The only people to act properly were John's disciples; and so light is cast by this story on the kind of courage that Jesus' disciples will require.

E) A WOMAN OF WIT (7:24–30)

An example of courage appears in the next woman we look at:

From there he rose up and went to the region of Tyre. And entering a house, he wanted nobody to know; and it was impossible for him to pass incognito. Instead, straightaway, a woman heard about him. Her daughter had an unclean spirit, and she came and threw herself at his feet. Now this woman was a Greek, Syrophoenician by race, and she asked him to expel the demon from her daughter. And he said to her, "Let the children eat their fill first, for it is inappropriate to take the children's bread and throw it to the house dogs." But she answered him, "Lord, even the house dogs eat under the table, from the children's crumbs." And he said to her, "Because of this remark, on your way—the demon has come out of your daughter." She went to her house and found the child in bed, and the demon gone.

This is an effortless and confident miracle; the question is not whether Jesus can do it, but whether he will do it for this person. The issue for Jesus is not whether miracles should be done for women; the assumption is that her gender is a matter of complete indifference to him. The issue is whether or not Jesus' mission extends beyond the boundaries of the people of Israel. For a good Jew like Jesus, hearing the call of God to remind Israel of what it used to stand for, it would hardly cross his mind that God's reign might also break into the world of the non-Jew. So Jesus is here confronting an issue of major importance for his own personal life and for his grasp of the mission on which he is embarked. His first instinct is to dismiss non-Jews as "house dogs," and to reserve his work only for the "children of the house." But the woman forces him to reconsider, not by bridling at the discourtesy of referring to herself and her daughter in such an uncomplimentary way, but by her ready wit.

Sometimes scholars suggest that in Matthew (whose version of this story we shall look at in the next chapter) the woman gets her way because of her faith, whereas in Mark it is because of her repartee. When it comes down to it, Matthew's view is probably not too different from that of Mark. For the purpose of our inquiry, the interest lies in the fact that it is a woman that Jesus is talking to. This woman believes in Jesus, stands firm before him, is not in the least put out by his disdain. She engages him in dialogue and persuades him, finally, to "see" her as a person rather than as the owner of the label "Gentile." This woman is the only person in the synoptic gospels to make Jesus change his mind. And we shall see in a later chapter that the only person in the fourth gospel to have that effect on Jesus is also a woman.

F) A QUESTION OF MARRIAGE (10:2–12)

Our next passage has Jesus' enemies laying a trap for him:

And some Pharisees approached and asked him if it is allowable for a man to divorce a woman. They were trying him out. He answered them, "What did Moses command you?" They said, "Moses gave permission to write a document of divorce and send her packing." Jesus said to them, "He wrote this commandment with an eye on your hardness of heart. However, from the beginning of creation, 'Male and female God created them. Therefore human beings will leave their father and their mother, and join their spouse, and the two shall be one flesh.' So that they are no longer two persons, but one flesh. Therefore what God has yoked together, let no human being separate."

In the house, his disciples raised this matter with him again. And he told them, "Whoever divorces his wife and marries another, commits adultery with regard to her. And if she divorces her husband and marries another, she commits adultery."

The question, as Mark makes clear, is a trap, and it may have been posed in order to persuade Jesus to say something indiscreet about Herod's domestic situation. The question of divorce was also, however, an issue apparently debated in the Judaism of Jesus' day. Jesus answers the Pharisees' question with a question to which he knows the answer, but which may force them to reconsider the basis on which they are posing the question. That basis is an entirely androcentric one, and Jesus removes it from under them by insisting that marriage cannot be undone. That must have been a shattering rewriting of the script of their world, and the disciples ("back in the house") are strikingly reluctant to accept the teaching. This reluctance prompts Jesus to restate the teaching even more forcefully: the alleged right of a man to divorce his wife is nothing less than legalized adultery. In the world in which Jesus moved and taught, this remarkably radical view will have worked for the protection of women against the arbitrary whims of husbands, for whom their wives were property and nothing more. For Jesus, women are undeniably equal human beings.

G) THE POOR WIDOW (12:41–44)

Jesus' gift for rewriting the conventional script is evident in the next story:

> And sitting opposite the Treasury, he observed how they were all putting spare change into it; and a good many of the rich put in a good deal. And a single poor widow came; and she put in a tiny sum, just two little coins. And he summoned his disciples and said to them, "Amen I tell you, this poor widow has put more than everyone else who put into the Treasury. For they all contributed out of their surplus, while she, out of her neediness, put in all she had, her entire life."

Once again, Jesus shows this extraordinary ability to see what is before him. We have to imagine a scene where donations are publicly and loudly recorded, and where men, the "breadwinners," will have been apparently the more meritorious simply because they gave more. Jesus, however, rewrites this script and highlights the woman's generosity. The woman who "put in her whole life" is the model disciple, imitating the Son of Man who, we have already been told, is "going to be killed" (8:31; cf. 9:31, 10:34), whereas the male disciples in various ways showed their inability to understand the demand for generosity in those who wish to follow Jesus (see 8:32; 9:33–34; 10:35–41). Mark does well to place this story right after the controversies of chapters 11 and 12, which make it clear that the battle lines are drawn, and that Jesus' death is now inevitable, and immediately before chapter 13's graphic account of a world that is falling apart. This woman represents, better than anybody we have seen so far in the gospel, the radically new way of being-for-God that Jesus represents and to which Jesus' disciples are invited.

H) A WOMAN ANOINTS JESUS (14:3–9)

Our next story belongs in the same context, only this woman is an even better model for disciples. This is a story that Mark evidently felt fitted so well as a commentary on the passion of Jesus that he inserted it between verses 2 and 10 of chapter 14. Notice how easily those two verses run into each other, but Mark places the story here because he wants us to pause and reflect on the Jesus who is going to his death. In reading this tale, it is helpful to reflect on the fact that the men, who seemed to be closer to Jesus than this unnamed woman, did not really grasp, as she did, what discipleship is about:

> And while he was in Bethany, at the house of Simon the leper, as he lay down to eat, a woman came in, with an alabaster jar of myrrh, of genuine precious nard. She broke the alabaster jar, and poured it over his head.
>
> Now some muttered indignantly, "What is the point of this waste of myrrh? [Because] this myrrh could have been sold for upwards of three hundred denarii, and given to the poor." And they denounced her harshly. Jesus however said, "Let her be. Why do you give her trouble? She has done a good deed for me. For you always have the poor with you, and whenever you want you can do good to them; but you do not always have me. She has done what she could: she anointed my body with myrrh ahead of time for my burial. Amen I tell you, wherever the good news is proclaimed in the whole world, what this woman has done will be spoken of in memory of her."

Once again, those last four words remind us that our (male-dominated) memory of this brave woman does not extend so far as the courtesy of remembering her name. However, we do and should recall, as Jesus here predicts, "what she has done." It is absolutely clear who the hero is, even if she is anonymous.

Like the widow to whom we have just had our attention drawn, she is utterly generous. She makes this "useless" gesture of love, which is also, fairly clearly, the act of anointing Jesus as Messiah. Like that widow and like all true disciples of Jesus, she performs a gesture that can be interpreted as "scandalous waste." The reproof about her failure to give to the poor is no more than an excuse, and Jesus' words might even be taken to imply that those who complained were in fact *not* giving to the poor, and that therefore their concern for the poor was fake and a debating expedient. The myrrh, foreshadowing a death, as well as confirming a messiahship (for Mark, Jesus is above all and always a *dying* Messiah) is, by contrast, utterly real and grounded in sober fact. This woman is the model disciple, strategically poised as the gospel launches into the passion narrative at which it has been aiming, certainly since chapter 8, and in another sense since its beginning. She exemplifies the loving generosity with which Jesus undergoes his passion and which we are called to show as disciples. Once again, the two questions, Who is Jesus? and What are his disciples like? are inseparable in Mark's gospel.

i) A Slave Girl Tells the Truth (14:66–70a)

Disciples do not always get it right, of course. Consider this next powerful tale:

> And while Peter was outside in the hall, a single one of the little slave girls of the High Priest came up. She saw Peter warming himself, looked straight at him, and said, "You were also with the Nazarene, that Jesus." He denied it, saying, "I neither know nor understand what you are saying." And he went out into the forecourt.
> And the slave girl, seeing him, again started telling those who stood near, "He is one of them." He denied it again....

This woman is not a disciple, but she tells a courageous truth in the face of a craven lie. We cannot but admire her spirit, while contritely recognizing our propensity rather to imitate Peter's cowardice than her honesty. In a telling gesture, Mark has Peter "warming himself." No one else appears to stand in need of heating, but then no one else is about to commit treachery. And Mark also depicts Peter as "on the run," as he "goes out into the forecourt." There is an almost comic touch (were it not so tragic) in the sight of this unnamed and presumably unimportant female trapping him in the truth.

j) Women at the Death of Jesus (15:40–41)

We should, however, remember in Peter's favor that he was at least there or thereabouts. The other disciples have not been seen since they disappeared in a fearful cloud of dust (14:50), including one who was so determined to leave Jesus to his fate that he left also all his clothing (14:51–52). Not so the women, however, as Mark admits to us only after it is all over:

> And there were also women looking from afar, among whom were included Mary the Magdalene and Mary of Jacob the small, and the mother of Joses, and Salome. These ladies, when he was in Galilee, used to be his disciples and deacons; and there were many other women who came up with him to Jerusalem.

These women are praiseworthy, although their existence and fidelity are only acknowledged by Mark grudgingly, when it is too late. In my translation, I have used the words *disciples* and *deacons,* where the Greek says that they "followed him and ministered to him," to indicate that Mark is using language here that was on the verge of becoming (if indeed it had not already done so) technical language within the early church. This was the fourth use of that verb *diakoneo* in the gospel, and it is, once again, women who are found doing it.

K) WOMEN AT THE BURIAL OF JESUS (15:47)

The faithful women were still there when Jesus was buried, witnesses to the site, even though their testimony would not stand up in court:

> And Mary the Magdalene and Mary of Joses saw where he was laid.

These two women model the true disciples of Jesus, who are faithful unto death, his or theirs. They challenge us to imitate them.

L) WOMEN AT THE (FAIRLY) EMPTY TOMB (16:1–8)

The same is true in the next passage, with which Mark's gospel originally ended (16:1–8):

And when the Sabbath was at last over, Mary the Magdalene and Mary of Jacob and Salome purchased aromatics, so as to come and anoint him. And extremely early on the first day of the week, they came to the tomb, when the sun had risen. And they were saying to themselves, "Who will roll the stone away from the entrance to the tomb for us?"

And they looked up [or: "they regained their sight"], and saw that the stone had been rolled away. For it was very big.

And going into the tomb, they saw a young man sitting on the right, wearing a white robe. And they were astounded. He, however, said to them, "Don't be astounded; you are looking for Jesus the Nazarene, the one who was crucified. He is risen, he is not here. See the place where they put him. But go and tell his disciples, and Peter, 'He is leading you [or: 'he is going ahead of you'] into Galilee. You will see him there, just as he told you.'" And the women came out and fled from the tomb, for fear and amazement held them. And they said nothing at all to anybody. For they were afraid.

This is a striking ending to the gospel, but it is undeniably odd. One can forgive those early Christians who thought that any good gospel should end with a proper resurrection scene and thus added various alternative endings to make up for Mark's perceived deficiencies. There are various points to notice here in our search for the women.

First, obviously, the women did not believe that Jesus had risen. If a body is to be anointed, it must be securely in the place where it was last put. Second, they show considerable and commendable courage in coming very early in the morning to the tomb, although Mark perhaps permits himself a little joke at their expense when he says that "the sun had already risen." He is not here referring to the time of day. There may also be a hint of mockery in his observation that they were wondering about getting the stone rolled away from the tomb. If the women did not at this stage believe in the resurrection, they were a good deal closer to the truth than the men. And so, in the next breath, Mark tells us that they did see, after all, for the word generally translated as "they looked up" can also mean "they saw again," as it does, for example, in the Bartimaeus story (10:52). Their outlook has been profoundly changed, as Mark perhaps means to indicate with his comment, "for it was very big."

Next, one should note the women's courage as they go into the tomb, for that is a dangerous place to be, especially if unpredictable things are taking place, such as stones being rolled away. Their courage is rewarded, however, by a thoroughly mysterious encounter, with a "young man," who is "sitting on the right," just as Jesus had indicated would be true of the Son of Man when we next saw him (14:62). The evangelist tells us that the women were "astounded," as well they might be. However, as God or the messenger of God characteristically does in biblical encounters, he tells them not to be astounded and then reveals prior knowledge of why they are in the tomb. Not only that, he also announces to them that the resurrection has taken place, and points to the place where Jesus had been, as evidence that at least the tomb is empty.

These same women are then given a commission: they are to be apostles of the good news to the disciples (and the young man goes out of his way to mention Peter, who had so energetically denied all knowledge of Jesus) and to reassure them about their mission into Galilee. This task is quite likely the most significant that could possibly be laid on a disciple of Christ. But then, according to Mark, the women are model disciples and can be trusted to perform their job.

Earlier it was noted that the women "went in" to the tomb. Mark now balances that carefully with the statement that they "went out," but then indicates that they failed to perform the task they had been given. They are terrified, he tells us, and "said nothing at all to anybody. For they were afraid." Some commentators argue that Mark ruins the whole gospel by depicting the women as predictably frightened and ineffective, and so he too slips into an androcentric vein.

Yet, if the women had the courage to go *into* the tomb in the first place, it is unlikely that we are to conceive of them as lacking the courage, on coming *out* of the tomb, to pass on the good news of Jesus' resurrection and that he is gone to Galilee. Imagine yourself a Christian in the late 60s of that first century of our era, listening to the gospel being read out for the first time after Mark has completed it. The evangelist or lector, clearly coming to the end of the scroll, concludes, as you listen, with the last sentence of the passage as I have given it, "...they said nothing to anybody, for they were afraid." What is your reaction? Is it not uppermost in your mind to say, "But they must have said something to someone. Otherwise we should not be sitting here!"? We need to savor Mark's gentle irony at this point. The women are indeed model disciples, and they were at the tomb, and they did convey to the frightened men, including Peter, the news that Jesus was no longer dead and that they would meet him on their mission. It is a well-judged ending to the gospel.

Conclusion

Where, then, are the women in Mark's gospel? It has been pointed out by scholars that there are no "women's parables" in Mark as there are in Matthew and Luke, but on the other hand, there are not many parables in Mark at all. Then, certainly, the women are not named in the list at 3:13–19, of those who were to "be with him, and for him to send them out to proclaim, and to expel demons." On the other hand, it can never be said of the women that they do not understand, and their hearts are hardened, as it is of the men (6:52), nor that they are "still mindless" (7:18), or do "not yet understand" (8:21). It is not the women who systematically misunderstand and reject Jesus' prediction of his own passion and death (8:32–33; 9:31–34; 10:35–41).

The women, by contrast, as the gospel develops, take on increasingly prominent functions, from the first one who after her cure "ministered to" Jesus, to those last who spread the news of the resurrection. It is the women, and not the men, who are the model disciples in Mark's gospel, which is part of the reason why some scholars argue that the Mark to whom I have been referring with a masculine pronoun throughout this chapter, may in fact have been a woman. So, to return to the second of those two questions which in my view the gospel sets out to answer, if you want to know what a disciple of Jesus should be like, according to Mark, look at the women.

CHAPTER FIVE

MATTHEW'S GOSPEL—A SERIES OF SHOCKS

NOW WE TURN TO MATTHEW'S GOSPEL. Until relatively recently it was the best known of the four, since it comes first in our New Testament and tended to be the one read most often in church. It is easy, therefore, to drift into the assumption that Matthew is a comfortable old friend; but even comfortable old friends can surprise us. If we read this "first gospel" with an open mind, there are a good many shocks awaiting us. Many of these concern the women whom we find in its pages, and at the end of this chapter I shall argue that for Matthew the women are those who know whom and how to worship.

Consider this saying which, except for the last sentence, is found only in Matthew:

> Don't you be called "Rabbi," for your Teacher is only One, and you are all brethren. Don't call anyone "Father" on earth, for your Father is only One, the heavenly one. And don't be called "guides," for your Guide is One, the Messiah.
> The greatest of you will be your servant [or: "deacon"]. Those who lift themselves up will be pushed down; And those who put themselves down will be exalted. (Mt 23:8–12)

Most people tend to slither—particularly those of us who are professionally addressed as "Father"—with some embarrassment past this saying, and that in itself is mute testimony to its shock value. If we take it seriously, however, there is no possibility of us setting out to build a patriarchal society and then claiming the sanction of this gospel for such an enterprise. It must be said that Matthew's gospel often seems to be addressing men only, but that may be because no one had thought of asking him whether he was addressing *all* Christian believers or simply the men.

78

Certainly the above quotation wholly discourages any attempt to construct a *basileia,* except the *basileia* of God. That word can be translated as "kingdom" or "empire," and it refers to any situation where an upper class or supreme individual lords it over the lower classes. This quotation clearly implies, according to Matthew's gospel, that everyone is on an equal footing in the new era that Jesus has inaugurated.

Not everyone would agree with this verdict. Some feminist scholars point out that Matthew's gospel begins with Jesus' family tree, which is quite clearly a "patrilineage," and ends with the commission to male disciples. Furthermore, it is argued, its best-known and loveliest section of teaching, the Sermon on the Mount, is apparently addressed exclusively to "men," "sons," and "brothers," not merely because this is grammatically inevitable, but also due to the very examples that the evangelist chooses. Nevertheless, women are also there in the gospel, at both its beginning and its end, and sometimes in unexpected and even shocking ways, certainly in ways that will not readily allow for a patriarchal reading of the text. As you read the gospel, look out for those moments of unexpectedness, the verses that point to a mysterious God who shatters all our categories, including the apparently obvious or "commonsense" category of male and female.

A) JESUS' ANCESTRY (1:1–17)

The gospel starts with a passage that is often discreetly overlooked—the genealogy of Jesus. It has been described as "the most boring bit of the New Testament," but is in fact a long way from being just a gentle and uncontroversial start to the Jesus story. For one thing, Matthew's neat division of the family tree into three groups of fourteen is not meant to make us admire a remarkable mathematical coincidence; instead, it is a proclamation that Jewish history, in all its promise and in all its vicissitudes, has found its completion in Jesus the Messiah. Genealogies are common in certain parts of the Old Testament, and on the whole women are not usually mentioned in these family trees except when they will be important later in the story. In Matthew's genealogy, however, no less than four women are mentioned, and this is no accident.

The four women are Tamar, Rahab, Ruth and "Mrs. Uriah." You can read their stories in Genesis 38, Joshua 2, the four chapters that compose the charming Book of Ruth and 2 Samuel 11–12, respectively. Why does Matthew choose those four? Various guesses have been made: the fact that they were all "foreigners" is one suggestion, or that they exhibited various kinds of sexual irregularity is another. Tamar pretended (for quite good reasons) to be a prostitute; Rahab certainly was one; Ruth managed to secure Boaz as her husband by somewhat unconventional late-night behavior; and Bathsheba was the hapless pawn in David's game of lust and murder. Some feminist scholars argue that all four are "outside the patriarchal system" and therefore proffer a challenge to it, thus emphasizing that God is not constrained to work through that system. That seems to me quite near the mark; my own preferred view (though I do not see a way of telling for certain what Matthew intended here) is that the women are presented because of the independence of spirit that each of them shows at various stages in their biblical narrative and which they share with Mary the mother of Jesus. At all events, Matthew is not simply embroidering casually; when he mentions these ancient heroines, he means us to see something, perhaps something shocking, about the way in which God operates in the history of Israel as it reaches its climax in Jesus. And we are required to bear that something in mind as we read through the rest of the gospel.

Another oddity that you may have observed is that Matthew also nullifies the whole genealogy by the manner in which he ends it. Having gone to all that trouble in tracking Jesus' ancestry through the menfolk stretching back to Abraham, he then renders it all pointless by concluding with "Joseph, the husband of Mary, of whom was born Jesus called Messiah," and in the next few verses asserting that Joseph was *not* the father of Jesus.

So right from the beginning of the gospel we are given a series of shocks to keep us on our toes and remind us that this is no ordinary story that we are following. This means that any overly-simple explanation of what is afoot is pretty well bound to be wrong.

B) JESUS' CONCEPTION (1:18)

With all this in mind, let us look at how Matthew relates the conception of Jesus:

Of Jesus Messiah the Genesis was after this fashion. His mother Mary being betrothed to Joseph, before they came together was found to be pregnant, by the Holy Spirit.

There is an extraordinary contrast here between the stilted solemnity of Matthew's Greek (which I have attempted, not altogether successfully, to render into a similar kind of English) and the tidings that it conveys. There are echoes, of course, of the opening of the gospel (see Mt. 1:1, with its reference to Jesus' "genesis," which itself echoes the first line of the Bible), but the news that Mary is pregnant by somebody other than Joseph is not at all what is expected in such a context. The slightly grudging concession at the very end of the sentence, that the child was "by the Holy Spirit," does not make it much easier to digest. Once again, it is important not to run away from the shock that Matthew wishes us to experience.

C) JOSEPH'S ROLE (1:18–2:23)

In this section, Mary is mentioned first. The son to be born is hers, not Joseph's, and Joseph's function, though vital, is quite secondary to her task of bringing into the world the one who is to be called Jesus. Joseph, in response to a dream-vision of the "angel of the Lord," takes the humiliating option of accepting Mary, along with her child who is not his. He performs the task of naming the child, as would be the norm in that society. Finally, Joseph, according to Matthew, abstains from intercourse with his wife prior to the birth of Jesus. For the evangelist, this is simply another way of asserting that it was not Joseph who fathered the child. Joseph is, there-fore, decidedly in a secondary role in comparison with Mary.

This is even clearer when some visitors arrive:

[The Magi] coming into the house saw the child, with Mary his mother, and falling down they worshiped him; and they opened their treasures and offered him gifts, gold and frankincense and myrrh.

The center of attention here, of course, is Jesus, and for Matthew these strange foreigners indicate what kind of thing Jesus' birth is simply by the presents they give, representing Jesus respectively as king, as priest and as destined for death. If that were not sufficient, then there is further cause for astonishment in the discovery that it was Oriental stargazers, rather than the local professionals and rul-ing classes, who first recognized the truth about Jesus. Even more striking is the fact that Joseph is nowhere to be seen, and the only person who witnesses this highly symbolic presentation of gifts is the baby's mother. It would be missing the point to observe that it is Joseph who dictates Egypt as the place to which they will flee and that Mary has no choice in the matter. Matthew's aim here is not to delve into the dynamics of the male-female relationships of the time, but to shock us with a dim apprehension of who Jesus really is.

This is how Matthew reports the end of the episode with the Magi:

And as [the Magi] went away, look, the angel of the Lord appears in a dream to Joseph, saying "Arise, take the child and his mother, and flee into Egypt, and be there until I tell you."

Once again, Matthew's mind is on Jesus. Mary has not much choice here, but then neither has Joseph, now in his second dream of the gospel so far, with two more to come. Matthew's main interest is in the startling notion that the "King of Israel" has to flee from his own people to Egypt, of all places, and by night at that, in a dreadful reverse of Israel's Exodus. As the evangelist continually reminds us, this is all a matter of fulfilling the Scriptures, which find their full meaning in Jesus.

D) JESUS AS WISDOM (11:19; 11:28-30; 12:42; 23:27-39)

There is in Matthew's gospel a tendency, which may go back before Matthew, to deal with Jesus as "Mother Wisdom." This is today referred to as "Sophia Christology" or "Wisdom Christology," and many feminist scholars have made profitable use of this idea in their approach to the question of who Jesus is. The word *Wisdom* is feminine in Greek, Hebrew and Latin, and the Old Testament personification of Wisdom is clearly a female figure. That figure is at certain points (see Proverbs 1:20-33; 8:1-36 and ben Sira 24) presented as the one who assisted in the process of creation and who was sent to live in Israel as God's emissary. The idea enables theologians to explore the mystery of Jesus in a way that does not stress the fact that he is male.

Our next three texts show something of this. The first is the passage about the comparisons made between Jesus and John the Baptist, to the discredit of both. John is accused of having a demon, while the charge against Jesus is that he is

a glutton and a winebibber, a friend of tax collectors and sinners. And [yet] Wisdom shall be justified by what she does.

The accusation is clearly quite a shocking one, but Jesus' answer shows a serenity in the face of the onslaught. Jesus as "Mother Wisdom" has much to teach us.

At the end of the same chapter Jesus again takes on the guise of Mother Wisdom and issues the following beautiful invitation (11:28-30):

Come to me, all you who labor and are burdened, and I shall give you rest. Take my yoke on you, and learn from me, that I am gentle, and humble of heart, and you will find rest for your souls. For my yoke is easy and my burden light.

There is in this text nothing of the aggressive posturing of a patriarchal society, but only a gentle, almost maternal, invitation. The response to the angry demand for "proof" and "authority" is simply "come and see." A slightly stronger form of this occurs in the next chapter, where Jesus responds in these terms to the scribes' demand for signs (12:42):

> The Queen of the South will rise up at the judgment [and do battle] with this generation and condemn it, because she came from the ends of the earth to hear the wisdom of Solomon, and, look, there is greater than Solomon here.

Feminist scholars who put weight on "Wisdom Christology" point to the Queen of the South as an example of a woman who comes, in no spirit of partisanship, looking for wisdom, crossing ethnic and gender boundaries to do so, while the men demand proof.

Our next passage (23:37–39) shows Jesus, rather charmingly, as Mother, and perhaps as Mother Wisdom:

> Jerusalem, Jerusalem, city that killed the prophets, and stoned those sent to her, how often have I wanted to gather your children, in the way that a bird gathers her brood; and you people were reluctant.

It is a well-observed and gentle image, not a condemnation, though its continuation foresees the inevitability of Jerusalem's destruction. Jesus' invitation is not a menacing matter of "Do this or else," but a summons to us to act in our own best interests.

E) THE EXECUTION OF JOHN THE BAPTIST (14:6–11)

But when there was a birthday party for Herod, Herodias's daughter danced in the middle; and she pleased Herod. So, with an oath, he declared that he would give her whatever she should ask for. Urged on by her mother, she said "Give me, on a dish, the head of John the Baptist." The king was saddened, because of the oaths, and because of those who were dining with him, and he ordered the request to be granted, and he sent and had John decapitated in the prison. His head was brought on a dish, and was given to the girl, who carried it to her mother.

This is obviously—and obviously meant to be—an unpleasant story, even in Matthew's account, rather briefer as it is than Mark's version. The two women are certainly not played as heroes; the hero is, of course, John the Baptist, who is off-stage throughout until his head appears on a dish. The villain of the piece is undoubtedly Herod, who is trapped by his admiration for a beautiful dancer, by his known bloodthirstiness, by the fact that he is in an incestuous marriage for which John had condemned him and by his desire not to lose face in front of his guests. The mother is not without blame: asking for someone's head, no matter what the provocation may have been, is simply a disgusting thing to do, and to that extent her daughter (who could have asked for something else) is an accomplice in the crime. Matthew is not, however, criticizing them as women, but as responsible human beings who have sacrificed their integrity. This is the story of every human being who ever got trapped in a sinful situation: it is partly caused by our own weakness and folly and partly the effect of something outside ourselves.

f) NOT COUNTING WOMEN? (14:21; CF. 15:38)

Our next, very brief passage has sometimes been misinterpreted as indicating that Matthew downgrades all but the men. This is partly because of an unlucky, though not incorrect, translation:

> And those who ate were about five thousand men, apart from women and children.

The Greek word that I have translated "apart from" also means "without" or "separately," and it has sometimes been put into English in this text as "not counting." Understandably, but not wholly accurately, some critics have argued from this that Matthew thinks that "women and children don't count, are unimportant." As a matter of fact, he has added them in where Mark (6:44) explicitly had only men, but it does underline how careful we must be in translation.

G) A WOMAN WHO MADE JESUS CHANGE HIS MIND (15:21-28)

Our next passage is a powerful one, and some scholars have found Jesus uncomfortably dismissive of the woman with whom he speaks:

> And going out from there, Jesus withdrew to the regions of Tyre and Sidon. And, see, a Canaanite woman from that area came out and shouted, "Have mercy on me, Lord, Son of David; my daughter is in a bad way with demons." But he didn't answer her a word. And his disciples approached and asked him, saying "Get rid of her, for she is shouting after us." He replied and said, "I was only sent to the lost sheep of the house of Israel." But she came and worshiped him, saying "Lord, help me." But he answered, "It is not proper to take the children's bread and throw it to the dogs." She said, "Yes, Lord, and yet the dogs eat from the crumbs that fall from the table of their Lords [or: "masters"]." Then Jesus answered and said to her, "O woman: great is your faith. Let it be done to you as you wish." And her daughter was healed from that hour.

This passage has puzzled quite a few people; and one can see why. The woman is a foreigner, a Canaanite according to Matthew, which is more or less what you might expect in Canaanite territory. The male disciples just want this public nuisance eradicated. Jesus himself is rather brusque towards her, or some would say, decidedly rude. According to at least some scholars, the whole story is just another way of reinscribing patriarchy. It can be read another way, however. Those who criticize the story do so on the supposition that all gospel stories have Jesus as their hero; but it seems that this may be one of those rare episodes where not Jesus but his antagonist is the hero.

There are a good many issues here, more than we have space to deal with in full, but consider at least the following: first, Jesus and the woman are both described as "going out," whereas Mark places the episode inside a house. Therefore, they are in public space, territory which is normally reserved for men, rather than the private space that was the women's quarters. On the other hand, geographically, it is the woman's territory because she is a Canaanite, which

Jesus certainly is not. So they are in a kind of sociological "No Body's Land." Then, secondly, the woman speaks beautifully in the language of the church: "Son of David, Lord have mercy on me." The only answer she receives, however, is an unresponsive silence on Jesus' part and a contemptuous "Get rid of her.... " from the disciples. This enlists the reader's sympathy on her side and against the men, especially the disciples, whose motives are clearly not commendable, nor commended. It also tends to turn sympathies against Jesus, who has to be prodded by them to take action and even then refuses in terms that cannot fail to be discourteous, despite the gallant efforts of some commentators to turn "dogs" into lovable pets, rather than something like "bitches" or "outcasts."

Against all that, is set the woman's persistence. She never loses her composure, but performs the right gesture by "worshiping" Jesus and, with a beautiful simplicity, begging, "Lord, help me,..." which earns her the dreadful remark about "dogs." Still she does not yield the argument, but turns Jesus' sword wittily back on him. And she *wins her point:* For Jesus addresses her with awed respect: "O woman!", an expression for which there is no parallel in the gospel and grants her, without any further argument, what she has been asking for.

The clue seems to be in Jesus' first response, which could also be translated, "I was not sent except to the lost sheep of the house of Israel." This story, in other words, as I argued when discussing Mark's version of this story, is about Jesus' own understanding of his mission. He had supposed that it was simply to Israel, but this woman has taught him otherwise. It is therefore a question more about who is to receive the good news than about the relations of men and women. It is a lovely story, and one for us to return to frequently in prayer.

H) A WOMAN WHO DID NOT MAKE JESUS CHANGE HIS MIND (20:20–28)

This story may be intended to shed some light on the tale of the Canaanite woman:

Then there came to him the mother of the sons of Zebedee with her sons, worshiping, and asking a favor of him. He said to her, "What do you want?" She said, "Say that these two sons of mine can sit, one on your right and one on your left in your kingdom." Jesus answered, "You lot do not know what you are asking. Can you drink the cup that I am about to drink?" They said to him, "We can." He says to them, "My cup you will drink, but sitting on my right and left is not mine to give. It is for those for whom it has been prepared by my Father."

Matthew has changed this from what he found in Mark, who had just the two boys make the request. Like the Canaanite woman, she "worships" Jesus and makes a request, though without the liturgical language. Unlike her predecessor, she does gain a response initially: "What do you want?" However, there is an important difference in that, as it turns out, she is not asking for the elimination of demons, but for help in a power game. So her request is not granted; instead another favor is granted, rather less welcome had they only understood what Jesus was talking about. "To drink Jesus' cup" means, of course, sharing in his death. The two brothers, to whom Jesus' response is clearly addressed, evidently do not understand a word of what he has been saying. So whereas in the previous episode Jesus met a reasonable request with initial discourtesy, in the present one, he treats with courtesy a request that turns out to be most unsuitable, given the quite unhierarchic nature of his program. And whereas the foreigner's request was in the end granted and gave us a deeper understanding of what Jesus was about, the Galilean woman's request is turned down because it has nothing to do with his aims. The focus of this story, therefore, is not on the inappropriate request made by the mother of James and John, but, more generally, on power relations within Jesus' group. It still carries a rather discomfiting message for us today.

I) THE TEN VIRGINS (25:1–13)

Then the *basileia* of Heaven will be like ten virgins, who took their lamps, and went out to meet the bridegroom. Five of them were foolish, while five were wise; for the foolish ones, when they took their lamps, did not take oil along with them, whereas the wise ones took oil in containers along with their lamps. The bridegroom was late, and all the virgins grew drowsy, then fell asleep. But in the middle of the night, a cry went up, "Look—the bridegroom! Come out to meet him." Then all those virgins woke up and decorated their lamps. But the foolish virgins said to the wise ones, "Give us some of your oil, because our lamps are going out." The wise ones answered, "No—there might not be enough for us and for you. Go instead to the people who sell it, and buy for yourselves." So off they went to buy, and while they were gone, the bridegroom arrived. And the women who were ready went with him into the wedding, and the gate was locked. Later on, the other virgins also arrived, and said "Lord, Lord, open up for us." He answered, "Amen, I tell you; I don't know you." Stay awake, therefore, because you do not know the day nor the hour.

The function of this story is, I suspect, to shock rather than teach the lesson, beloved of preachers, about foreseeing every possibility. Apparently the fault of the excluded virgins is that they were unprepared for a wholly unexpected delay (for bridegrooms are not normally late for their own weddings). Despite the last verse, their fault is *not* that they fell asleep, for all the girls did that. We may also feel some sympathy for the foolish; the wise were, after all, a shade ungenerous, as it seemed that the bridegroom really was coming any minute now, so they could surely have spared a drop or two. The wise virgins are displaying a hardness of heart, and we cannot feel at ease in taking their side. And the bridegroom, too, is surely not above criticism. When he says that he does not know the latecomers, we may feel that all he had to do was open the door or even look through the spy hole, and he could *see* who it was on the other side.

Perhaps the moral here is not that we should hoard against a rainy day, nor that we should stay awake; instead, I think that the moral is in the shock. God does not act in our ways, and will not be dictated to by human reason. Some feminist scholars are inclined to emphasize the androcentricity of this passage; but I think the point is that Jesus' new enterprise is a startling one, and that a new kind of society is being formed.

J) THE ANOINTING AT BETHANY (26:6–13)

Our familiarity with the passion story may blind us to its surprising aspects, but Matthew and his readers well knew the text in Deuteronomy 21:23, "...cursed be the one who hangs on a tree." That is perhaps why, like Mark, he puts the following tale, which is electrifying from start to finish, right at the beginning of his passion narrative:

> When Jesus was in Bethany, in the house of Simon the leper, a woman approached him holding an alabaster jar of valuable myrrh, and poured it on his head as he lay there. The disciples saw it, and were cross. They said, "What's the point of this waste? For this could have been sold for a large amount, and given to the poor." Jesus understood and said, "Why do you give her hassle? For she has done a good deed by me. For you always have the poor with you, but you do not always have me. For when she flung this myrrh on my body, it was in aid of my burial. Amen I say to you, wherever this good news is preached in the whole world, what she has done will be spoken of in memory of her."

Those last four words, as I have already said, comprise the title of a famous work of feminist biblical scholarship, the ironical point being that we have in fact forgotten the woman and do not even know her name. Note also the following points: first, Jesus is in a leper's house, and therefore outside the pale of normal society; second, he is approached by a woman and does not in any way resist this likely source of defilement; third, whatever way the gesture is interpreted, it is undeniably an odd thing to do uninvited—to pour oil, no matter how valuable, over a man's head. This is underlined by the disciples' horror, which, not for the first time in this gospel, presents them in an unsympathetic light. Contrast that with Jesus' gentle reaction, and it is clear that, once again, the woman is the hero of the story, anonymous though she may be.

There is a further oddity about the passage that is not often noticed. Observe that no less than four sentences begin with the word "For." In other words, there is an argument going on, but the arguments do not seem all that strong. The first is the argument of the disciples: the oil should not have been poured in this extravagant way because it could have been given to the poor. There is nothing wrong with this argument as such; Judaism preached open-handedness to the poor, and Jesus was certainly at ease with the poorest classes. But it is not the final word on this particular episode, and we must be prepared to walk on unfamiliar territory that shifts beneath our feet.

Let us look now at Jesus' arguments. The first is that "she has done a good deed by me," which would suggest that extravagant gestures towards Jesus are of a higher priority than generosity to the poor. This is intended to shock the reader into thoughtfulness. The same is true of the second argument, which has occasionally been unworthily seized upon by those who wish to avoid our obligation of concern for the poor: "...you always have the poor with you, but you do not always have me." We need to take a deep breath as we hear this line of reasoning and recall the fact that Jesus is about to die. The third argument reinterprets the woman's gesture. On the face of it, her action has all the marks of an anointing, so that what she is doing is proclaiming Jesus as Messiah. Jesus does not deny that in what he says, but rereads that action as "for my burial." In other words, most shocking of all, this Messiah is a dying Messiah. Like the parable of the ten virgins, the function of this story is to startle us into an awareness of who Jesus is and what his ministry involves.

K) PETER AND A LITTLE SLAVE GIRL (26:69–72)

The next women we meet compare very favorably indeed with a particular man:

> But Peter sat outside in the hall; and there approached him a little slave girl who said "You were also with Jesus the Galilean." He denied it before everyone, saying "I don't know what you're saying." He went out to the gate, and another woman saw him, and said to those who were there, "This person was with Jesus the Nazarene." And again he denied with an oath, "I don't know the fellow."

There is no doubt about who the hero is in this terrible story. It was not the free man, but the single, unfree slave girl, who courageously told the truth. Matthew expresses her lack of resources in a way that is not easy to put into English. Not only is she powerless, but she is also absolutely correct, whereas Peter is committing public perjury and betraying a friend, having earlier promised that same friend, at 26:35, that "even if I am obliged to die with you, there is no way I'll ever deny you"! Moreover, as his move to the gate indicates, not only is he in denial, he is also in flight.

L) PILATE'S WIFE (27:19)

Our next woman, from quite the other end of the social scale, again surprises us:

> As [Pilate] sat on the judgment seat, his wife sent to him saying, "Have nothing to do with that innocent person. For I've suffered a lot today in a dream because of him."

The last dreamer that we encountered in the gospel was Joseph, and in his case we are told that the dream-messenger was "the angel of the Lord." Matthew, the only evangelist to include this episode, gives us no such information here. There is no doubt, however, that he regards her, like Joseph, as correct in her interpretation of the dream: Jesus *is* an innocent man, and this woman, like the one who anointed him a chapter or so ago, is well aware of that fact.

M) THE WOMEN AT THE CROSS (27:55–56, 61)

At this point in the text one has to look fairly hard to discover people who are on Jesus' side. The disciples have all fled (26:56), apart from Peter, who, as we have just seen, energetically denies any acquaintance whatever with Jesus; but now the evangelist brings into focus Jesus' women supporters, and there are quite a lot of them:

> There were there many women, looking from a long way off, who had followed Jesus from Galilee, to minister to him. Among them were Mary the Magdalene, and Mary the mother of James and Joseph, and the mother of the sons of Zebedee.

In Jesus' hour of greatest need, according to the evangelist, it was not the men who were there, but the women, some of whom are not anonymous and all of whom are described as "ministering" or "deaconing" to him. Notice that they include the mother of James and John, whom we last saw being smartly turned down when she was asking a question about power on behalf of her ambitious sons. Her presence at this (literally) crucial moment must be taken to atone for a thousand attempts at gaining influence.

Nor did the women then melt out of the scene; they remained obdurately there to the end, after Jesus was buried (61):

And they were there, Mary the Magdalene, and the other Mary, sitting in front of the tomb.

This loving fidelity, apparently useless though it may be (but how else would they have known where he was buried?) clearly meets with the evangelist's approval, for the story could not have reached its glorious climax without them.

N) THE WOMEN AT THE TOMB (28:1–10)

The last scene of Matthew's gospel portrays the male disciples, just as its first part listed Jesus' largely male ancestors; but the women make one more appearance. While they do not conclude the gospel, it is nevertheless they who inaugurate the new dispensation. Without them the men simply would not have known where to look:

Early in the week, as it was dawning on the first day of the week, there came Mary Magdalene and the other Mary to look at the tomb. And, look, there was a great earthquake. For the angel of the Lord came down from heaven and approached and rolled away the stone, and sat on top of it. And his form was like a shaft of light, and his clothing white as snow, and for fear of him, those guarding the tomb quaked, and became like corpses. Then the angel spoke to the women, "You are not to fear, for I know that you are looking for Jesus who was crucified. He is not here, for he is risen, as he said. Come and see the place where he was put. Then quickly go and tell his disciples that he is risen from the dead, and, look, he is going before you into Galilee. You will see him there. Look, I have spoken to you."

And they went quickly away from the tomb, in fear and great joy, and they ran to inform his disciples. And, look, Jesus met them, saying "Rejoice." And they approached and held on to his feet and worshiped him. Then Jesus says to the women, "Don't be afraid. Go and tell my brothers that they are to go off to Galilee, and there they will see me."

This is a remarkable ending, even if it is not quite the end. The two women are those who were last seen sitting outside the tomb, and they return to the same place, though Matthew does not vouchsafe to us any more than that they intended to "look at it." Then, however, God takes over in the person of the "angel of the Lord," whom we last saw addressing Joseph and telling him to accept Mary and her child. Now that child is dead; or, rather, not dead. And Matthew dryly points out that the guards, who had been posted precisely because there had been talk of a corpse rising from the dead (cf. 27:63–64), are themselves the ones who are behaving like corpses.

The women, by contrast, are quite undaunted by the supernatural manifestations and are in perfect condition to receive the message that they are given. Not only that, but they obey their instructions; and their reward, as they hurry away from the tomb towards their terrified male counterparts, is an encounter with the risen Jesus himself. They are greeted by him (what I have translated "rejoice," for obvious reasons, is also a fairly conventional salutation, such as "hail" or even "greetings") and given a job to do, the same as that which the angel had given them. It is worth noticing, however, that when the men finally meet with Jesus on the appointed mountain in Galilee, they only half recognize him ("they worshiped him; but they doubted", 28:17 [or : "but some of them doubted"]), whereas the women have not the slightest doubt about who Jesus is. What is more, it is the women who bring the gospel back to Galilee, where it more or less started, and the women who are the first to see the Risen Jesus. Matthew's gospel gives a markedly exalted role to the women.

Conclusion

We have seen that the gospel of Matthew is in many ways very shocking. The evangelist expects the following of Christ to involve the rewriting of conventional family relationships (see, for example, 10:21), so Matthew cannot be taken as simply "reinscribing patriarchy" even if the Sermon on the Mount is of little help for those who are looking to find the women. We have seen, in many of the episodes in which women are involved, that the evangelist frequently intended to startle us, although we may tend to overlook that shocking element in our reading of the text, just because it is so familiar to us.

There is one last point. Occasionally in the course of this chapter, I have mentioned the word "worshiping," translating thus a word that can also be rendered "falling prostrate" or "doing homage." This theme first arises in chapter 2, where the Magi propose to worship the newborn king (2:2) and eventually succeed in doing so (2:11). Herod uses the same verb for what he intends to do (2:8), but we know that he means something quite different and altogether more murderous by it. The next time it is employed is at 4:9, where the devil invites Jesus to "worship" him. Jesus refuses. After that, it is used once in chapter 18, where it describes the action of the unforgiving servant who is trying to get off his vast debt (verse 26). *All* the other uses of the verb describe people's approach to Jesus; and we already know from chapter 2 that it is a correct approach. There are seven of these uses. A leper in 8:2 asks for a cure; the synagogue ruler (9:18) wants his daughter brought back to life. At 14:33 the disciples in the boat worship Jesus after Peter's unsuccessful attempt to walk on the water, and at 28:17 the eleven worship Jesus, though not, as we have just seen, without misgivings. All the other instances—15:25 (the Canaanite woman), 20:20 (the mother of James and John) and 28:9 (the two Marys)—are of women showing reverence. Matthew's gospel thus pays early tribute to the fact that again and again in the history of the church it is the women who have shown the deepest faith in Jesus.

CHAPTER SIX

THE WOMEN IN THE FOURTH GOSPEL—
A STUDY IN CONTRASTS

JOHN'S GOSPEL IS AN EXTRAORDINARY PIECE OF WORK, one that a distinguished scholar has described as "a pool wherein an infant may paddle, or an elephant swim." It has a deceptive simplicity and an alluring complexity, as it invites the reader to make pilgrimage into the mystery of who Jesus is. In terms of the quest to which this book is committed, I shall be arguing that the women characters in the fourth gospel consistently "get it right," even more than those we looked at in the gospel of Mark, and that this is particularly evident when they are compared with the men around them. As before, I shall offer a translation of what seem to me to be the relevant passages and make some comments, which are not intended to be everything that could be said about each passage, but which may help in our search for the women in question. This gospel is generally supposed to be the latest of the four; but it seemed good to take the fourth gospel at this point, and so to let Luke-Acts, the subject of the next chapter, lead us into the world of St. Paul and the early church.

A) THE WEDDING AT KANA (2:1–12A)

And on the third day, a wedding took place in Kana of Galilee; and the mother of Jesus was there. Jesus was also invited, and his disciples. And when the wine ran out, the mother of Jesus said to him, "They have no wine." And Jesus said to her, "What does that concern either of us, woman? My hour has not yet come."

His mother said to the "deacons," "Whatever he says to you, do it." There were six stone water jars lying there, according to the purification rites of the Jews, up to two or three nine-gallon measures each. Jesus said to them, "Fill the water jars with water." And they filled them right to the top. And he said to them, "Now draw it out and take it to the head waiter." And they did so, and when the head waiter tasted the water, which had turned into wine–and he had no idea whence it came, but the "deacons" knew, those who had drawn the water–he addressed the bridegroom, "Most other people set out the best wine first, and the inferior stuff when people are drunk. You have kept the best wine until this moment."

Jesus did this as the first of his signs in Kana of Galilee, and revealed his glory, and his disciples believed in him. After this, he went down to Caphernaum, himself, and his mother and his brothers and his disciples....

The story starts "on the third day," and although there are a number of such indications of time in this gospel, the attentive reader who hears that phrase could hardly avoid thinking ahead to the resurrection, and reading the story in that context. Secondly, the reader might notice that this is a "wedding." In the synoptic gospels, the notion of the "wedding feast" is frequently invoked as a metaphor of what God is doing in Jesus' ministry. We find it so used also in this gospel, on the lips of John the Baptist (3:29-30). We may reasonably expect, therefore, to discover that this is more a story about who Jesus is than specifically about the women.

Nevertheless, we notice also that the story could not have happened without the presence of a woman, namely Jesus' mother, who appears only twice in the fourth gospel, anonymously on both occasions. We meet her here, where she sets his ministry on its way, and at the end (19:25-27), where she is asked to preside over its continuation. Moreover, the text makes it clear that she *belongs* at the wedding, whereas Jesus and his disciples are only *invited*. And this woman, whom we are meeting for the first time in this gospel, turns to Jesus and says, evidently expecting some response, "They have no wine."

Jesus' answer is apparently unenthusiastic. We should not, however, be led by our own cultural presuppositions into thinking that he is being rude here, for Jesus uses the same form of address to her again at 19:26, where clearly there is no hint of discourtesy. He also

addresses the Samaritan woman in this way at 4:21, Mary Magdalen
at 20:15, as the two angels have done two verses earlier, and the
woman taken in adultery (8:10), although, as we shall see, this story
was probably not originally part of John's gospel. The only other
character addressed thus in the vocative case in the fourth gospel is
the one whom he calls "Father." So rather than discourtesy, we may
be intended here to find a certain intimacy.

Clearly Jesus' first instinct is to resist the implied invitation, and
he strikes a somewhat discouraging note, as we shall see him doing in
the conversation with the Samaritan woman (4:7,16). The reason for
his resistance is interesting, though. He says, "My hour is not yet
come." In John's gospel, Jesus' "hour" is the climax of his ministry,
the cross, which is also the moment of his exaltation and of the gift
of the Spirit. Given that Jesus' resistance is rapidly overborne, we
may be right in seeing this episode as a foreshadowing of that climax.

In any case, Jesus' mother does not appear too discouraged,
because she tells the "deacons," "whatever he says to you, do it." I
have opted for the slightly tendentious translation "deacon" instead
of "servant" for two reasons. First, the Greek word used is *diakonoi*,
from which "deacon" comes, and which, as I have already indicated,
was certainly at this stage in the history of the church well on the
way to becoming a technical term for a hierarch. Second, "Do whatever he tells you" is not a bad motto for disciples, and we have
already seen reason to suppose that disciples are invited to be "deacons" or "servants."

It seems pertinent to our inquiry that it is a woman who is giving
the orders in this highly significant setting. Not only does she give
the orders; she has no doubt that Jesus is going to do something, for
she orders the servants or deacons, "Do whatever he tells you." The
evangelist leaves us to suppose that some nonverbal transaction, a
mutual understanding "between the lines" of their dialogue, has
taken place.

So Jesus gives the appropriate instructions, including the order
to "draw out," using a form of the word that will be used in the story
of the Samaritan woman to refer to the drawing of water (4:7,11).
The evangelist notes, quite undramatically, that the water has

turned into wine and has been passed on for the headwaiter's wine-tasting. Possibly the most significant term here is "whence" ("he had no idea *whence* it came"). This word is something of a key term in John and refers to the impenetrability of Jesus' origins for those who are not "in the know." Jesus' mother, though, is clearly "in the know" and will not be at all surprised, we deduce, by what actually happens. It is she who has instigated this "first of his signs" that "revealed his glory," and whereas we are told that "his disciples believed in him" nothing is said of his mother in this respect. Possibly this is because we are to understand her as already having the faith that is required of disciples in this gospel.

A final significant detail may be gleaned from the order of names in the last verse: the story started with the mention of Mary, Jesus and the disciples. By the end, the order has changed. Jesus has now done the "first of his signs," and the list, as they move from Kana to Caphernaum, reads: "Jesus, his mother, and his brothers and his disciples." This unnamed woman, who did not need to *come* to faith in him because she had it already, is named second after him, and ahead of the disciples, as she will be again at the crucifixion.

Jesus' mother contrasts with the "disciples" in general, but she contrasts profoundly with Nathanael, the last individual disciple whom the reader has encountered (1:45–51). Nathanael made a dismissive reply ("from *Nazareth* can anything good come?") whereas Jesus' mother shows a quiet confidence. Nathanael comes to faith ("Rabbi, you are Son of God, you are King of Israel") while the mother already has it. Finally, Nathanael starts by performing a Jewish ritual ("under the fig tree") while Jesus' mother has the effect of persuading her son to go beyond the Jewish purification rites to inaugurating a new world.

b) The Samaritan Woman (4:1–42)

Our next passage, a very long one, also shows a woman who out-does disciples in awareness of who Jesus is. This woman journeys in faith, it is true, but she outstrips the disciples on this particular part of the journey. It may help, as we read this passage, to remember that the whole of the fourth gospel is a journey into the mystery of who Jesus is. Above all, this woman is, for the evangelist and for Jesus, her partner in the dialogue, a person in her own right. Since the passage is so long, I shall divide it, somewhat arbitrarily, into paragraphs and put comments at the end of each such section:

> So when Jesus realized that the Pharisees had heard that Jesus was making more disciples and baptizing them than John (even though Jesus himself did no baptizing; it was his disciples who baptized) he left Judaea and went off back into Galilee.

This is a baffling beginning to the story. The evangelist wants Jesus to move from Judaea to Galilee, but it is never quite clear why, even when we come to the cure of the royal official at the end of chapter 4. By the time we reach the beginning of chapter 5, the action is once more in Jerusalem. Furthermore, nothing in the text so far indicates why a discovery on the part of the Pharisees about Jesus' baptismal practices should constitute a motive for flight. Finally, the evangelist contradicts himself on the matter of whether or not Jesus did any baptizing (rather as Paul does, oddly enough, at 1 Corinthians 1:14–17). Scholars offer various explanations of the oddity, such as a multiplicity of sources clumsily pasted together. The effect of this tangled introduction is to make us enter into the story itself with a sense of having emerged from dense jungle into the open plains.

> It was necessary for him to go through Samaria. So he came to a city of Samaria called Sychar, near the place which Jacob had given to Joseph his son. And Jacob's well was there. So Jesus, weary from the journey, sat down, just like that, at the well. It was about midday [*literally:* "the sixth hour"].

The well here is almost a character in this story, rather as the Temple functions at certain points in Luke's gospel. Jesus is going to meet a woman at this well, and in Scripture when man meets woman at such a place the upshot is generally a betrothal. We notice, too, with a slight sense of surprise, that Jesus is "weary." Nothing in the gospel so far has led us to expect such a thing. The word used for *weary* also means "having labored hard," which is important because one of the themes of this story has to do with the nature of apostolic labor. Finally, we notice the time: it is noon, a time when women do not go to the well. The evangelist may wish us to see her as marginalized in some way or other.

> There came a woman out of Samaria to draw water. Jesus said to her, "Give me to drink." For his disciples had gone into the city in order to buy food. So the Samaritan woman said to him, "How is it that you, a Jewish man, ask for a drink from me, who am a Samaritan woman?" (For Jewish males have no kind of intercourse with Samaritan women.)

Now at last appears the woman we have been waiting for. She has, as they say in baseball, two strikes against her. She is a woman, first, and, second, she belongs to the Samaritans, whose mixed ancestry and dubious practices have for some centuries rendered them ill-at-ease with their southern neighbors. To this double outsider (albeit in her own territory) Jesus makes a remark that is decidedly abrupt: "Give me a drink." This has a harsh ring to it, and it is not what we were expecting. The turn of events seems puzzling, as, very likely, the evangelist intends it to be, and this sense is not lessened after we are offered what purports to be an explanation: "*For* his disciples had gone into the city,..." but which actually explains nothing.

At last, though, with the woman's spirited and independent-minded response, pointing to the racial/cultural and gender boundaries over which the story is wandering, she comments on the oddity of what Jesus is up to. The sentence in parentheses underlines the strangeness. The ambiguity in the English phrase "to have intercourse," although it has moved of late more in a sexual direction, is there also in the Greek. Once again, the evangelist is signaling to us, so it seems to me, that we *ought* to find the whole thing rather peculiar. This is the last time, however, that Jesus' gender is brought to our attention in the story. Instead, the conversation drifts in the direction of the metaphor suggested by the *contents* of the well:

Jesus answered, "If you knew the gift of God, and who is the one who says to you, 'Give me a drink,' you would ask him, and he would give you running [*or* "living"] water." She said to him, "*Kyrie*, you have no bucket, and the well is deep. So whence do you have this running water? Are you—can you be—greater than our father Jacob, who gave us the well, and himself drank from it, and his sons, and his livestock?" Jesus replied to her, "Every man who drinks from this water will be thirsty again, while every man who drinks from the water which I shall give him, will never thirst, for all time; instead, the water I shall give him will become a well of water in him, which bubbles up to eternal life."

Jesus' reply, using the metaphor of "running" (the Greek can also mean "living") water, turns the conversation in an unexpected direction. It now becomes a revelation of who Jesus is, continuing the enterprise on which the whole gospel is engaged. There is an element of role reversal present here. Jesus is offering to take on the woman's role of water provider, and, by contrast, quite soon the woman will desert her bucket, which is the mark of that function. Jesus never gets the drink for which he asked. Yet both of them go away satisfied.

The woman shows herself more open than anyone so far in the gospel to a dawning Christological insight. There are three clues to this: first, she calls him *Kyrie*, which I have left in Greek, because it is an ambiguous term used both as the ordinary address to a man of even slightly superior class, as well as the proper address of Christians to the one they recognize as Lord. Second, she uses that word *whence*, which, as already noted, is such an important idea in the fourth gospel, hinting at a realm other than the present one where Jesus and his authority originate. Third, she sketches the almost unimaginable possibility that she might here be dealing with one "greater than our father Jacob."

One other point to notice about this passage is that although our only two characters at present are one male and one female, all the endings that Jesus uses in his reply about drinking the water that he will give are *masculine*. In one sense, of course, this is entirely proper. The masculine in Greek includes the feminine where both are intended, but in terms of our inquiry it is striking, and I have slightly emphasized the incongruity by translating the masculine as such.

> The woman said to him, "*Kyrie,* give me this water, so that I may not thirst, nor come by here to draw water." He said to her, "Go, call your husband and come here." The woman replied, "I have no husband." Jesus said to her, "You have spoken correctly in saying 'I have no husband'; for you have had five husbands, and the one you have now is not your husband." The woman said to him, "*Kyrie,* I see that you are a prophet. Our fathers worshiped on this mountain, whereas you people say that in Jerusalem is the place where worship should go on." Jesus said to her, "Trust me, woman; the hour is coming when you will worship the Father neither on this mountain nor in Jerusalem. You people worship what you do not know; we worship what we know, for salvation is from the Jews. But the hour is coming, and is here now, when genuine worshipers will worship the Father in spirit and in truth. For indeed the Father seeks for men like this as his worshipers. God is spirit, and those who worship him must do so in spirit and truth." The woman said to him, "I know that Messiah is coming, the one spoken of as 'Christ.' When he comes, he will tell us everything." Jesus said to her, "*Ego Eimi,* the one who is speaking to you."

At last the episode reaches the major Christological revelation towards which it has been feeling its way for some time now. See how it is built up: first, the woman once again calls Jesus *Kyrie,* and the demand for water indicates that she uses the term in its higher sense of "Lord" rather than "Sir." Second, the revelation is made possible only by way of an apparently abrupt change of direction— the request to bring her husband. That may serve to remind us that the story presupposes the thoroughly patriarchal society in which both the gospel was written and in which this event is supposed to have taken place. More important, though, it enables the woman to go further on her Christological journey, which is interpreted twice subsequently ("he told me everything that I have done") as holding up a mirror to her.

The revelation of who Jesus is cannot, for the fourth evangelist, be separated from questions about who the reader is. Let me add, however, that this text carries no hard evidence other than the later avowal that "he told me all I did" for the sinful life that is frequently attributed to the Samaritan woman by exegetes. To have had five husbands may be a sign, not of wickedness, but of misfortune; and there is nothing in the text to suggest that her relationship with the present "man," who is not her husband, is in any way improper. He might, for example, be an aged relative. Certainly, the story is not presented as being primarily about the woman's sin and subsequent repentance.

Of greater significance is the fact that the woman, addressing him now for a third time as *Kyrie,* categorizes him confidently as a prophet. And on that basis, with another apparent switch of direction, she engages him in a theological discussion. The subject of this discussion is one that she has initiated, one that is relevant to the purpose of the gospel as a whole; and it leads to the conclusion that, because of what is going on as we watch, the religious distinctions between *Samaritan* and *Jew* are irrelevant. The woman attributes to Jews a view about the "place" where worship is to be done. Now in the Psalms the Hebrew word for "place" often means "the Temple," but in the rabbinic writings, all of which were codified after the destruction of the Temple, it is often used to refer to God. We are eavesdropping here on a profoundly theological discussion in which Jesus and the woman are partners.

Once again, I have somewhat emphasized the grammatically masculine endings in the translation. The reason for this is my sense that the barriers that separated the woman from Jesus—the barriers of race and gender—are here being looked at for the last time in the narrative in order that they may then be dismissed as irrelevant. They are irrelevant because of the continuing journey into who Jesus is. The woman perseveres with the journey, building on the firm foundation of her successful identification of Jesus as "prophet," by raising another category, which she does not yet directly apply to Jesus, namely that of Messiah. The reader, of course, knows already that this is quite precisely to be applied to him and so applauds the direction of her theological investigations, which get closer to the mark than anything else we have seen in the gospel so far.

Jesus' response underlines this. It is the first use in the gospel of a phrase that functions almost as a divine title in John, echoing God's self-description to Moses in Exodus 3. I have left it in Greek as *Ego Eimi*, which means "I am," but as the fourth evangelist employs it, can range from the banal "that's me" to a very important claim indeed (see, for example, 8:58), which might best be rendered as "I AM."

At this point in the story and with considerable artistry, the evangelist leaves the woman gazing into the depths of the mystery and focuses instead on the disciples, who are hardly scratching at the surface:

> At this, his disciples arrived; and they were shocked that he was talking to a woman. None of them, however, said, "What do you want?" or "Why are you talking to her?" So the woman left her pitcher and went into the city and said to the people, "Come here and see a fellow who told me everything I have done. Do you think he can be the Anointed One?" They came out of the city and went to him.

Notice the contrast that the evangelist paints: we and the woman have been on the verge of getting close to the heart of the mystery of Jesus, and the disciples trample all over the mystery as they purse their lips and mutter about the proprieties. There has been nothing at all untoward in the passage so far (rather the reverse). Nor anywhere else in the gospel is there an indication that Jesus ought not to be talking to women even though this one is a Samaritan. Furthermore, the encounter is at the socially meaningful location of a well. As far as the evangelist is concerned, any impropriety is the invention of the disciples. Nor do they quite know what to say, though the gospel indicates what they would *like* to have said; and it had nothing to do with the real heart of what has been going on.

While the disciples scratch their heads, the woman is no longer present. Significantly, she has abandoned the "tool of her trade," the pitcher with which she was going to draw the water (the same word, incidentally, as the evangelist used in 2:6,7 at the wedding in Kana), and has gone off to pursue another trade, that of evangelist or apostle. Like John the Baptist (1:8, 27, 29–34, 36), Andrew (1:41–42), and Philip (1:45–46), she focuses the attention of others on Jesus and raises the vital question of Jesus' identity, suggesting that perhaps he is the Messiah. As the Baptist has done for his two disciples, and as Philip has done for Nathanael, so the woman does for her fellow Samaritans. She arouses in them sufficient interest for them to pay Jesus a visit, which will in turn lead to further Christological discovery. The disciples, however, are still unaware of the discoveries that lie just beyond their grasp:

> Meanwhile the disciples were interrogating him, saying "Rabbi, eat." But he said to them, "I have food to eat that you are unaware of." So the disciples said to each other, "Do you think someone has brought him something to eat?" Jesus said to them, "My food is that I should do the will of the one who sent me, and accomplish his work. Do not you say, 'Another four months, and the harvest is on its way'? See, I tell you, lift up your eyes and just look at the fields: they are *already* white for the harvest. The one who reaps gets a reward and gathers fruit for eternal life, so that sower and reaper may rejoice together. For the saying is for real, that 'the sower and the reaper are different people.' I have sent you to reap where you have not labored. Other people have labored, and you have taken over their labor."

It seems no accident that the evangelist carefully places the woman's apostolic work between the two passages that show the disciples at their suspicious or uncomprehending worst. Her achievement is thereby thrown into high relief. This provides a nice example of what scholars call "Johannine irony." The disciples want to know whether he has had something to eat. In fact, he has not even had the drink that he originally asked for, but for him "food" is to do the Father's bidding; food is the apostolate on which the woman has already embarked. The disciples think that there are another four months to the harvest, but the woman has already acted. The fields are ready for harvesting *now*, and she is "gathering fruit for eternal life." The word translated as "labor" is the same word which at the beginning was rendered as "weary" when Jesus first sat on the well. Apostolic labor is in some sense its own reward. Now we see the fruit of that labor:

From that city many of the Samaritans believed in him because of the woman's remark when she testified, "He told me everything I have done." So when the Samaritans came to him, they asked him to stay with them, and he stayed two days. And many more believed through his word. And to the woman they said, "It's no longer because of what you said that we believe. For we ourselves have heard and we know that this is indeed the Savior of the World."

For the effect of the woman's remark we might compare the sayings at 17:20 ("those who believe in me because of their word," though the Greek word *logos* is used in a slightly different sense here) and 20:29 ("happy are those who have not seen and yet have believed"). What followers of Jesus have to do is talk about him to others, make suggestions about who Jesus might be, lead them to Jesus and then see if they will drink. Notice how carefully this is expressed in the final sentence, with "the woman" in the emphatic position at the beginning, and the title, "Savior of the World," to which the episode has led the reader, in the emphatic position at the end. The woman has done her job, and done it well. She has "sown," and others have "entered into her labor."

In John's gospel, the function of apostles is to bring others to Christ and then watch how they go "beyond the evidence." Two good examples of this "going beyond the evidence" are Nathanael at 1:49 and Thomas at 20:28. Certainly the woman here is a remarkable apostle, and the evangelist delicately points out the contrast with Nicodemus in the previous chapter. He arrived "by night," whereas she is there at noontime. He hardly understands a word, whereas she follows some very difficult theological conversation and even asks one or two penetrating questions of her own. She brings others to Christ, but nothing of the sort is said of Nicodemus. This woman can function as a role model for a disciple. Nicodemus cannot. Here is a good passage to be prayed over by those looking for the women in this gospel.

c) THE WOMAN TAKEN IN ADULTERY (7:53–8:11)

This episode, in the view of many scholars, should not be considered here. Many good early manuscripts do not place it at this point, and, what is a less objective criterion, it does not particularly sound like the writing of John. Nevertheless, it is considered at this point because 1) it is there and 2) if we are to talk about Jesus and women we can hardly omit examination of it at *some* point in the course of this book. It is a lovely story, and we should be the poorer without it:

> And they went, each to his own house; but Jesus went to the Mount of Olives. In the early morning, he went back to the Temple, and the whole crowd came to him. He sat down and taught them. Now the Scribes and the Pharisees brought a woman who had been arrested for adultery. They put her in the middle and said to him, "Teacher, this woman was arrested in the very act of committing adultery. Now in the Torah, Moses commanded us to stone women of this sort. So what is your view?" They were saying this to test him, so as to have grounds to accuse him. Jesus looked down and with his finger wrote something down on the ground. But as they persisted in their interrogation of him, he looked up again and said to them, "Let the sinless one of you be the first to throw a stone at her." And again he looked down and wrote on the ground. When they heard this, they went out one by one, beginning from the elders. He was left alone, along with the woman who was in the middle. Jesus looked up again and said to her, "Woman, where are they? Did no one condemn you?" She said, "No one, *Kyrie.*" Jesus said, "Nor do I condemn you. Go, and from now on, sin no more."

This powerful scene depicts a very public contest organized by the "Scribes and Pharisees." This designation is a rather loose umbrella term for Jesus' opponents. The story implies that for them the woman's misdeed is of small interest by comparison with the opportunity to entrap Jesus. However, there is someone missing; we should not be looking just at the unfortunate woman. If the woman was caught in the act of adultery, then at least one other party, and that one male, must have been present. The woman, however, is the only one on display, and she is put "in the middle," as the story twice emphasizes. Quite correctly, they are able to quote Torah on the subject (see Leviticus 20:10 and Deuteronomy 22:22–24), except that Torah says that *both* adulterous parties are to be put to death, and here in the Greek the opponents of Jesus speak only of the sentence being for "women like this," as though male adulterers were treated with impunity.

The point of the trap is to set Jesus against Moses. For this purpose, the woman is in the unfortunate position of a goat tethered in a jungle clearing in order to entice a tiger into an ambush. Jesus will not, however, be so enticed, and he writes on the ground, the only writing attributed to him in his entire ministry. Scholarly speculation on what he wrote has been abundant and fertile, but the story does not encourage us to speculate. It is a highly effective dramatic device showing indifference to his plight and, since there are two acts of writing, serving as a kind of "frame" for his verdict. The verdict is that the first to throw the stone should be the one without sin. Jesus bends down again and leaves them to it, and, powerfully, they file away "beginning with the elders."

Then Jesus, when the crowd has gone, can deal with the woman. And whereas for Jesus' opponents she was little better than bait, for Jesus she is a person, and she is accordingly engaged in dialogue, "Where are they? Does no one condemn you?" She makes her answer, and he his, a beautiful one that we *all* long to hear, "Neither do I condemn you. Go, and from now on, sin no more." The distasteful episode is utterly transformed and redeemed by the profound interaction of this man and this woman.

d) Theological Dialogue With Two Women (11:1–44)

Our next passage is ordinarily called "The Raising of Lazarus," and that is indeed what happens at the end. But the heart of the story is in Jesus' relations with two women and, more particularly, in what is revealed in the two conversations that form its center. Like the dialogue with the Samaritan woman, it is extremely long, so I shall highlight some points for consideration after each of the sections into which I have divided it.

And someone was sick, Lazarus from Bethany, from the village of Mary and Martha her sister. It was Mary who anointed the Lord

with myrrh and dried his feet with her hair, whose brother,
Lazarus, was sick.

Like the dialogue with the Samaritan woman, this story has been
given a very cumbrous introduction. It starts with the mention of
sickness ("lack of strength" would be a more precise translation),
and deceptively focuses our attention first on the sick person. The
story is not really about him, however, but about the two women to
whom Jesus reveals himself in the course of the episode, and we
need to remember at all times that the fourth gospel is a progressive
revelation of who Jesus is. There is nothing in the story to suggest
any revelation to Lazarus.

Another oddity, reminding us of how much we must read the
whole gospel together, is the reference to Mary anointing Jesus and
drying his feet. That has not yet happened in the unfolding of the
gospel story, but will take place in the next chapter, apparently in
part as a way of thanking Jesus for the fact that Lazarus has been
restored to life. We need to take this story with 12:1–8 and the
important details provided in 11:45–57, which are given special
emphasis by their position in between the two episodes.

> So the sisters sent to him saying, "*Kyrie*, look, the one you love is
> sick." When Jesus heard this, he said, "This sickness is not going
> to end in death; it is for the glory of God. Its purpose is to glorify
> the Son of God."

The action here is initiated by the sisters. We notice also that the
evangelist has previously described Bethany as "the village of Mary
and Martha," giving them a prominence that they at no point lose in
the telling of the story. Jesus' reaction to the message is striking, and
the evangelist intends it to be. He speaks of "the glory of God" and
of "the Son of God." "Glory" is a key term in this gospel, and should
warn us again that the story is part of the progressive revelation of
who Jesus is, and of his relationship to God. In addition, since in
John's gospel "glory" refers at least occasionally (12:23, 28, 43;
13:31, 32; and perhaps 17:1, 5, 24) to the death of Jesus, we must be
on the lookout here for the strains of the Passion.

Jesus loved Martha and her sister and Lazarus. **Therefore** when he heard of the sickness, he stayed where he was for two days. Then, after this, he said to the disciples, "Let's go back to Judaea." The disciples said to him, "Rabbi, only recently the Judaeans were looking to stone you, and you are going back there?"

In this section I have bolded the word *therefore* to indicate that in my view it is the most bizarre use of this strong logical connective in the entire New Testament. The evangelist is, characteristically enough, sending us a signal that if you understand who Jesus is and his relationship to God, you "march to the beat of a different drum." This drum taps out a rhythm that leads to death: the step Jesus now takes leads towards his execution, or as John's gospel understands it, his "glorification."

Jesus answered, "Aren't there twelve hours in the day? If a person walks in the day, they do not stumble, because they see the light of this world; but if they walk in the night, they stumble, because the light is not in them. He said this; and then he said to them, "Lazarus our friend has fallen asleep; but I am going in order to wake him up." So his disciples said to him, "*Kyrie,* if he has fallen asleep, he will be saved." Jesus had referred to Lazarus's death, but they thought he was referring to Lazarus as really asleep. So then Jesus said openly to them, "Lazarus is dead. And for your sakes I am **delighted,** so that you may have faith, that I was not there. Come, let's go to him."

Jesus points out, accurately enough, that there are only twelve hours of daylight, but the attentive reader of the gospel knows also that there is only one "hour" (which had not come at 2:4, but has arrived by 12:23) and that hour is coming precisely as a result of this episode. The "light" of which Jesus speaks is thematic to the gospel. Indeed, John's gospel can be seen as a battle between the light and the darkness, and the idea of "light" has to do with the gradual uncovering of Jesus' true identity. The "word" was identified as the "light" in the gospel's prologue (1:4–9), and chapter 9 is a prolonged meditation on what it means to call Jesus the "light."

The disciples in this passage, however, do not seem over-endowed with light. As so often in the gospels, and as we saw in the story of the Samaritan woman, they blunder about here. We are invited by the evangelist to compare these disciples with the theologically far more adroit women with whom Jesus will shortly hold dialogue, both of whom know that Jesus has power over death. Once again, I have bolded a word. It is ordinarily translated as "rejoice," but here has been rendered "delighted" to draw the reader's attention to its oddity. It makes sense only insofar as we grasp that the heart of the story, the purpose of the whole gospel, is the continuing journey into who Jesus is.

> So Thomas, the one known as "Twin," said to his fellow disciples, "Let us go too, so as to die with him." So when Jesus got there, he found that Lazarus had already spent four days in the tomb. Bethany was quite near Jerusalem, about a mile away, and a number of Judaeans had gone out to Martha and Mary, to comfort them for the loss of their brother.

Jesus' puzzling delay turns out to have made no difference. He had postponed his departure by two days, but Lazarus has been dead for four days. Even the most expeditious setting-forth would not have kept him alive. The sense that we get throughout the fourth gospel, that Jesus all the time knows precisely what is going on, is therefore deepened, and Thomas's uncomprehending resignation ("let us go and die with him") only serves to highlight it.

> So when Martha heard that Jesus was coming, she went to meet him; Mary sat at home. So Martha said to Jesus, "*Kyrie,* if you'd been here, my brother would not have died. Still, even at this stage I know that whatever you ask of God, God will give you."

As Mary will subsequently (and in the selfsame words), Martha here greets Jesus with what is unmistakably a reproach. We, the readers, know that insofar as the reproach is leveled at his delay in setting off, it is not justified. Nevertheless, we listen in as this woman addresses her challenging question to Jesus and notice also how her disapprobation is rapidly swallowed up in a declaration of faith. Not only does she call him *Kyrios,* but she also indicates that, through him, God is in charge of the whole episode. She is therefore equipped for the revelation that is to follow, just as the openness of the Samaritan woman prepared her as well for the discovery that Jesus was Messiah.

> Jesus said to her, "Your brother will rise." Martha said to him, "I know that he will rise at the resurrection on the last day." Jesus said to her, "*Ego Eimi* the Resurrection and the Life. Whoever believes in me, even if they die, shall live; and everyone who lives and believes in me will not die a permanent death. Do you believe this?" She said to him, "Yes, *Kyrie.* I believe that you are the Messiah, the Son of God, the One who is coming into the world."

The Samaritan woman received her revelation in the form of the near-divine title, which we saw might be translated as "I AM," and now Martha receives an even more exalted version of it, not just "I AM the Messiah" but "I AM the Resurrection and the Life." It is a daring thing to say in the face, not only of Lazarus's death, but, as we are becoming increasingly aware, of Jesus' own death. The reader knows, however, that this daring declaration does not go further than the facts permit.

The brisk and revelatory dialogue concludes with the vital question, enabling us to check whether Martha is one of "his own," to whom Jesus came (1:11): "Do you believe this?" And Martha makes a massive statement of faith, going beyond the evidence before her, and declaring in ringing tones that Jesus is "...the Christ, the Son of God, the One who is coming into the world." This is the equivalent in the fourth gospel for what the synoptic evangelists put on the lips of Peter, as the highest Christological formulation by a disciple prior to the resurrection (see Mt 16:16 for the closest parallel, and compare Mk 8:29, Lk 9:20). Once more it is a woman to whom the evangelist allots this theologically significant utterance.

This interchange with Martha, together with the following dialogue between Jesus and Mary, forms the heart of our episode. It is taken as a revelation of who Jesus is. The conversation with Martha brought out Jesus' status before God; when he talks to Mary we learn something quite different:

> And as she said this, she went off and called Mary her sister and told her discreetly, "The teacher is here, and he is calling you." When Mary heard, she arose quickly and went to him. Jesus had not yet entered the village, but was still at the spot where Martha had met him. So the Judaeans who were with her in the house, consoling her, seeing Mary rise up quickly and go out, followed her, supposing that she was going to the tomb to weep there.
>
> So when Mary came to where Jesus was, and saw him, she fell at his feet, saying, "*Kyrie*, if you had been here, my brother would not have died." So when Jesus saw her weeping, and the Judaeans who had come with her also weeping, his emotion was intense, and he was disturbed, and he said, "Where have you put him?" They said to him, "*Kyrie*, come and see." Jesus wept. So the Judaeans said, "See how he loved Lazarus." But some of them said, "Couldn't this fellow, who opened the eyes of the blind man, prevent Lazarus from dying?"

While the dialogue with Martha was private, this is altogether a more public affair. It starts out, deceptively, with the same question, but asked with reproach. This miniepisode is given a quite different context by the gesture with which Mary greets Jesus: "...she fell at his feet...." This alters the tone of the story, and reveals something quite different about Jesus. The conversation with Martha carried what you might call direct theological revelation, whereas here the revelation (against the background of the discreet word in Mary's ear, the speed with which she went to Jesus and the crowd of keeners who went with her to weep) is that Jesus is a person affected by emotion; the phrase translated as "he was disturbed" literally means "he disturbed himself." Here the focus is no longer on Jesus' theological significance, but, equally revelatory, on his human feelings.

This part of the story culminates in that moment, astonishing at least in this gospel, when Jesus is shown the place where Lazarus was buried: in three Greek words, perhaps even more telling in the briefer English version, "Jesus wept." The emotion is made more intense by the muted clucking, part motherly and part a little bit

hostile, of the "Judaeans" in the background, but forms an unforget-
table counterpoint to the lofty sentiments of the dialogue with
Martha. This other woman, her sister, has been the means of com-
pleting a remarkable revelation about Jesus, and this scene sets up
the comparatively undramatic conclusion of the episode, the actual
raising of Lazarus.

> So Jesus, again in the grip of intense emotion, came to the tomb.
> It was a cave, and a stone lay in front of it. Jesus said, "Remove the
> stone." Martha, the dead man's sister, said, "*Kyrie,* he is already
> stinking, for it is the fourth day." Jesus said to her, "Did I not tell
> you that if you believe, you will see the glory of God?"

Before death yields up its prisoner, however, Jesus stands at the
tomb showing both the emotion that the dialogue with Mary had
engendered, and at the same time, that he is the Figure-from-
Another-World whom Martha had discerned. The cave and the stone
have the reader looking ahead to Jesus' own burial, and the authoritative command to "remove the stone" is a harbinger of what will
come nine chapters hence. For the seventh time in this episode, Jesus
is addressed as *Kyrie,* though our grasp of the term has gone a good
deal deeper now. Then he uses Martha's severely practical utterance
as a springboard into theological revelation about the "glory of
God," and we are reminded again that God is to be glorified, para-
doxically enough, by Jesus' death. After that mind-stretching conun-
drum about the divine, the end of the story is almost an anticlimax:

> So they removed the stone. Jesus lifted his eyes upwards and said,
> "Father, I thank you that you have heard me. I knew that you hear
> me all the time, but because of the crowd standing round, I said it,
> so that they may believe that you sent me." And saying this, he
> shouted in a loud voice, "Lazarus, come out here." The dead man
> came out, bound hand and foot with strips of cloth, and his face
> was bound round with a face cloth. Jesus said to them, "Undo
> him, and let him go."

This seems almost, but not quite, an anticlimax. Jesus places the
whole episode in context with a final and characteristic prayer to

the Father and utters the command to Lazarus, who as though it were the most natural thing in the world, effortlessly obeys. The whole thing seems so easy that we almost fail to notice that he is wearing grave cloths and a face cloth.

The whole story now turns and rushes towards the death of Jesus. The evangelist outlines the consequences in the verses which come after (11:45–57), which may be summarized as follows:

- some Judaeans believed (45)
- some informed the Pharisees (46)
- the Sanhedrin debated the matter, fearing the loss of political independence, or rather, the loss of Temple and nationhood (47–48)
- Caiaphas unwittingly analyzes the situation correctly (49–52)
- the decision (long foreseen by Jesus and by the reader) is reached to bring about Jesus' death (53)
- Jesus retires to somewhere near the desert (54)
- in view of the imminent Passover and the excitement about Jesus, the "high priests and Pharisees" give orders for his arrest (57).

This remarkable story is not really about these two women in particular, nor about women in general, but about the revelation of who Jesus is, particularly in the face of death, both his own and another's. Nevertheless, two women are shown at very great length as partners with Jesus in dialogue. Martha has a profounder understanding of who Jesus is than anyone in the gospel so far and is then led even deeper into the mystery. Mary is the means of revealing to us the emotions that we might not otherwise have suspected in the one whom the gospel has described as "Word," "Son of God," "Son of Man," "Messiah" and so on. Without her, we should have had less grasp of what it means to say that "the Word became flesh" (1:14).

These two women have enabled us to see the significance of the episode in the larger picture that the gospel endeavors to draw. The theological and personal sensitivity of these two women stand in stark and favorable contrast to the head-scratching confusion of the disciples, the banalities of the crowd and the homicidal intent of the religious establishment. This passage should be read closely with the one that now follows.

e) The Anointing at Bethany (12:1–8)

So Jesus, six days before the Passover, came to Bethany, where Lazarus was, whom Jesus had raised from the dead.

So they had a meal in his honor there, and Martha was "deacon," and Lazarus was one of those who lay down to eat with him.

So Mary, taking a pound of myrrh, pure nard, very valuable, anointed the feet of Jesus and with her hair dried his feet. The house was filled with the scent of the myrrh. Judas Iscariot, one of his disciples, who was about to hand him over, said, "Why was this myrrh not sold for three hundred denarii and given to the poor?" He said this, not because he was worried about the poor, but because he was a thief, and looked after the money box, and removed what was put into it.

So Jesus said, "Leave her alone; let her keep it for the day of my burial. The poor you always have with you, but you do not always have me."

This passage drives the story forward to the Passover, when a new paschal lamb is to be sacrificed, and links it back to the previous episode, which was also a victorious encounter with death. Four times the evangelist uses the strong Greek word for "therefore," which I have in each case translated as "so" and, slightly artificially, used to mark off a separate paragraph. Certainly the third use, which introduces the anointing that is the core of this story, is the oddest of the lot, making this highly unconventional action seem as though it were the most natural thing in the world. For a moment the evangelist allows us to concentrate on the beauty of this loving gesture and to sense his approval of what is going on, even including the charming detail that "the house was filled with the scent." Then he sets up the contrast, perhaps just a shade clumsily, as he puts the negative view on the lips of Judas Iscariot, "who was about to hand him over." As though this were not enough to discredit anything he was about to say, the evangelist makes the inconsequential and somewhat vindictive remark by way of a gloss that "he said this...because he was a thief."

Judas may or may not have been a thief. One gets the impression that the early church would have believed anything at all of the one whom they saw as "betraying" Jesus. But giving to the poor is a sensible notion, well within the accepted practice of both Judaism and Christianity, and one need not be a thief in order to argue for it. The evangelist is here setting up Judas as anti-hero, contrasting him with the "Ideal Shepherd" (10:1, 8, 10) in order to throw Mary's heroism into more profound relief and to indicate that she and Jesus, unlike Judas, both knew what was going on.

Jesus confirms this by giving the fairly sharp order to "leave her alone" and then the exhortation to "let her keep it for the day of my burial." This is more mysterious in that it is not clear whether it is the oil (which presumably is by now pretty well irretrievable) or the loving gesture that is to be kept. Either way, the woman is vindicated, and we are again reminded that Jesus' death is now imminent, less than a Sabbath away. The discerning reader will further observe that I have once again made the slightly tendentious translation of "deacon" to describe what Martha was up to on the grounds that the first readers of John's gospel were quite likely to have picked up the reference to an ecclesial office. Both women, therefore, figure here in prominent and positive light.

F) "WOMAN—BEHOLD YOUR SON" (19:25-27)

There stood by Jesus' cross his mother, and the sister of his mother, Mary of Clopas, and Mary the Magdalene. So Jesus, seeing his mother standing by, and the disciple whom he loved, said to his mother, "Woman—behold your son." Then he said to the disciple, "Behold your mother." And from that hour, he took her to his own.

Even though the evangelist never names the mother of Jesus, the episode is very striking. For any mother to be at a son's deathbed is a terrible reversal of what might normally be expected. When that deathbed is the violent and undignified execution that the Romans awarded to slaves, even though this evangelist makes the cross more of a royal throne than a gibbet, the poignancy is increased. For our purposes it is striking that those of his intimates named as present at the death of Jesus were women (perhaps as many as four of them), and that the sole male is the "beloved disciple," who in any case emerges slightly stealthily from the background.

So the woman who initiated the first of Jesus' signs attends also the last of them and is part of the assurance that his near-to-last royal act is not in fact the end of the Jesus story. For by this gesture a royal dynasty is set up, over which the mother of Jesus presides. The beloved disciple takes her "to his own," as the evangelist reminds us that the Word incarnate also came "to his own" (1:11), not all of whom received him. The mother of Jesus and these other women and all who respond with an understanding of what is happening here are part of the future of the story of Jesus.

G) MARY MAGDALENE GOES TO AND FROM THE TOMB (20:1–18)

The last passage in the fourth gospel in which women figure is by no means the least important:

On the first day of the week, Mary the Magdalene came early, while it was still dark, to the tomb, and saw the stone taken from the tomb. So she ran and came to Simon Peter, and to the other disciple, whom Jesus loved, and said to them, "They have taken the *Kyrios* from the tomb, and we do not know where they have put him." So Peter and the other disciple went out and came to the tomb. The two of them ran together; and the other disciple ran ahead, at a better pace than Peter, and got to the tomb first. And he stooped down and saw the linen cloths lying, but he did not go in. So then Simon Peter also arrived, in his wake, and he went into the tomb and saw the grave cloths lying, and the face cloth, which had been on his head, not lying with the other cloths, but rolled up apart, in one particular place.

So then the other disciple also went in, the one who had got to the tomb first. And he saw and he believed. For he had not yet come to faith in the text that Jesus must rise from the dead. So the disciples went back to them.

But Mary stood by the tomb, weeping outside. So as she was weeping, she stooped down into the tomb, and saw two angels sitting in white, one at the head and one at the feet, where the body of Jesus had lain. And they said to her, "Woman, why are you weeping?" She said to them, "They have taken away my *Kyrios,* and I do not know where they have put him." As she said this, she turned round backwards, and saw Jesus standing there, and didn't know that it was Jesus. Jesus said to her, "Woman, why are you weeping? Whom are you looking for?" Now she thought he was the gardener, and said "*Kyrie,* if it's you that have taken him away, tell me where you have put him, and I'll remove him." Jesus said to her, "Mary." She turned round and said to him in Aramaic, "*Rabbouni,*" (which means "Teacher"). Jesus said to her, "Don't touch me, for I have not yet ascended to the Father. But go to my brothers and tell them that I am going to my Father and your Father, to my God and your God."

Mary the Magdalene went and told the disciples, "I have seen the *Kyrios,*" and that he had said these things to her.

The story of this last faithful witness, the woman who came first to the tomb and then waited for long enough by it after the men had gone to discover the final truth about Jesus, is a powerful one. There is a little more to come in the gospel—Thomas has yet to make his climactic pronouncement (20:28); the evangelist has still to tell us what was his purpose in writing the book (20:31), not to mention the whole of chapter 21, where we learn what is to become of Jesus' disciples. Nevertheless, this woman's witness is the final piece in the theological puzzle that the evangelist has been endeavoring to help us solve.

We cannot help contrasting her with Peter, whose verdict on the empty tomb is not known at this stage, and with Thomas, who still requires another piece of evidence before he will believe (20:25), or even with the Beloved Disciple, who is said to have believed, but not to have done very much about it except go home. Certainly the evangelist draws attention to Mary's bravery in going to a tomb while it is still dark and therefore, in her culture, very likely to harbor demons. She finds the Lord absent, but has at this stage no inkling of the explanation, and runs off to the male disciples.

First we get a puzzling, and slightly comical, not to say undignified, episode where one man arrives at the tomb before the other. This may, as scholars argue, reflect a power struggle in the early church. On the other hand, it may not; certainly it cannot be read as eliminating all female contribution. It is true that the Beloved Disciple, but not, apparently, Simon Peter, "sees and believes," going "beyond the evidence." But both of them seem to feel that at that point they have done enough.

Mary, by contrast, stays on at the tomb, faithfully weeping, as Jesus had at another tomb not many chapters earlier, which suggests that the evangelist invites us to praise her. She sees what Peter and the Beloved Disciple did not see, namely two divine emissaries who refer, not unkindly, to the fact that she is weeping. And we notice that all the way through the episode she steadfastly refers to Jesus as *Kyrios,* which may indicate that she still has some sort of theological grip on the rather puzzling situation.

Then, and because of her fidelity, she finds Jesus. Admittedly, she rather stumbles into him, but find him she does, the first person to do so since his death. Again the question about weeping is put to her, with the familiar and more penetrating question, "Whom are you looking for?" Then comes a splendid piece of Johannine irony, for she accompanies her misidentification of Jesus as the gardener with the address of *Kyrie,* which if offered to a passing gardener would be an appropriate politeness, but when spoken to Jesus, as properly understood in the fourth gospel, is theologically a very weighty title indeed.

Once she has been addressed by name, she triumphantly makes the identification for which we have been waiting and of which the men are still presumably uncertain, "*Rabbouni.*" Then she is given a mission—to be the "apostle to the apostles." Finally, the last sentence of the episode with the solemn beginning by way of the title "Mary the Magdalene" draws our attention to her faithful performance of the mission.

Conclusion

The fourth evangelist's treatment of the women is sympathetic. By contrast with the other actors in the story, they show profound insight into the identity of the Jesus revealed in this gospel. The women seem to get to the heart of what it means to be a disciple of Jesus: they come to faith in him; they act as apostles; and in a number of different ways demonstrate precisely the qualities that the evangelist expects to find in Christian disciples.

In addition, though not here considered, it seems to me that in the "Last Discourse," which occupies such a substantial portion of the second part of the gospel (chapters 13–17), it would be possible to argue that Jesus is portrayed as Mother. The saying at 16:20–22 on the pains of giving birth is quite without parallel in our literature. The emphasis on love from the first verse to the last of these chapters—the astonishing action with which they open (the washing of the disciples' feet by Jesus), the mention of the Beloved Disciple and the fact that he lies in Jesus' lap, the desire not to leave them as orphans (14:18)—all serve as a counterweight to the androcentric and patriarchal impression that can be given by the gospel's use of male pronouns for God and for the human race and the identification of God as "Father." Read with proper care, it seems to me, this material undermines patriarchy and offers a vision of a world in which, under God, all human beings are equal, for "all those who received [the light], he gave them the authority to become children of God, those who believe in his name, who were not born of blood, nor of the will of flesh, nor of the will of a man, but were [simply] born of God" (1:13).

CHAPTER SEVEN

LUKE-ACTS— "AN EXTREMELY DANGEROUS TEXT"

IN THIS CHAPTER WE SHALL DEAL WITH the two-volume work, known as "Luke's Gospel" and the "Acts of the Apostles" or "Luke-Acts." You could go the length and breadth of a fairly sizable biblical conference nowadays without encountering anyone who thinks that the two works have a different author, and if you want a quick introduction to the reasons why this is so, just look at the first four verses of each work to see the similarity of style and address.

In neither case is the title, either "The Gospel of Luke" or "Acts of the Apostles" quite accurate. I have already explained that we have no particular grounds for saying that the author was someone called Luke, and the author does not call his first volume a gospel. Instead, he announces his intention of "writing everything accurately in order, having gone into it from the beginning." And "Acts of the Apostles" is not an account of the doings of the twelve apostles, nor of the much larger number of persons who seem to have had that honorable title in the early church, but of two of them—Peter, in the first part, and in the second, Paul, who was not one of the Twelve, but who receives far more of our author's attention.

The description of Luke-Acts in the title of this chapter as "an extremely dangerous text" is not my own, but that of a distinguished feminist biblical scholar, Jane Schaberg. Her reason for calling it dangerous is that, at first reading, Luke appears to be very "woman-friendly," for he includes a good many women in his narrative. They appear in no less than forty-two passages of the gospel, twenty-three of which are in the material found in Luke alone and for that reason known by some scholars simply as "L."

123

These passages include many of the most charming stories that we know, such as the stories of Elisabeth and Mary, the account of Jesus' birth and infancy, the narrative of Martha and Mary and the dinner at their house. The trouble is that we can all too easily be seduced by Luke's very charm.

Of all the evangelists, Luke is certainly the most artistic story-teller; his is the pen that gave us such stories as the Good Samaritan, the Prodigal Son, Zacchaeus, and the Ten Lepers. The argument is that Luke's very charm may blind us to the fact that he sees the role of women as one of docile subordination, so in his two-volume work they do not say very much but simply get on with the job of looking after the men and being obedient to them. Some scholars argue that Luke's stance with regard to women is closest to that of the Pastoral Letters (1 and 2 Timothy and Titus) that we shall be looking at in chapter 9. It is also suggested that Luke represents a stage when the church is adapting to what is expected of it in the Roman world, drifting away from its Jewish roots and perhaps learning to disparage those roots.

One point to consider is that at times Luke seems to present men and women in pairs. If that is so, then presumably women and men are equal in the evangelist's esteem. Have a look at the following passages in Luke's gospel to see what I mean: 13:18–21 (the parables of the mustard seed and the leaven); 15:4–10 (lost sheep and lost drachma); 7:12–17 (the widow's son at Nain) with 8:41ff (Jairus's daughter); 13:10–17 (the cure of a woman on the Sabbath) with 14:1–6 (cure of a man on the Sabbath); 6:12–19 (men named as disciples and men healed) with 8:1–3 (women named as disciples and healed). Furthermore, Luke's is accurately described as "the gospel of social justice," which would necessarily include justice to women. You may notice, as we go through the two volumes, the number of times widows are mentioned, and widows are a prime example of those who suffer in a male-dominated society.

We should not, however, press our defense of Luke beyond what can itself be defended. There is a remarkable number of women mentioned by name in his two volumes, but they are not seen in roles of leadership and represent fewer than half of the names mentioned. Some feminist scholars regard it as typical of Luke that he omits the story of the Syrophoenician woman, whom we meet in the gospels of Mark and Matthew. But she is a part of Luke's "Great Omission" of all the material from Mark 6:45–9:50, which provides one explanation.

At all events, you can see that we are considering a question of very great complexity, on which there are several different views. One scholar has suggested that those who think that Luke takes a negative view of women are the ones who look "through" the text at the church of Luke's day and place, while those who take a more positive view concentrate more on the way in which Jesus behaves in the gospel.

Inevitably, since I hold to the view that the same author wrote both Acts and Luke, I shall frequently blur the distinction, and have indeed already blurred it, between the two volumes. For convenience, however, I am going to treat them separately and in order of their appearance in the New Testament.

1. LUKE'S GOSPEL

At the beginning of this gospel you might notice some disturbing clues about how to read the text. Read the first four verses, with their elaborate formality and their air of beginning a history book, and see how that seems to carry on into verse 5:

> In the days of King Herod of Judaea, there was a certain priest named Zachariah of the quotidian of Abijah, and his wife was of the daughters of Aaron, and her name was Elisabeth.

Then, however, the tone changes, and we see that Luke was not primarily interested in the list of names, but in portraying the last two as a couple in whose lives God is about to intervene:

> They were both just in the sight of God, walking blamelessly in all the commands and regulations of the Lord. And they had no child, because Elisabeth was barren, and they were both advanced in their days.

Luke is signaling to us that things are not quite what they seem in this text. It may *look* like history; in *fact* it is a story of God's work in human life.

In case we had not quite grasped it, Luke repeats the pattern at the beginning of the next chapter. It starts:

> And it happened in those days that a decree went out from Caesar Augustus that the whole world was to be enrolled. This enrollment was the first that was done when Quirinius was Governor of Syria.

Once again, this has an impressive solemnity, with the mention of the emperor and his local representative (although there is something of a muddle over dates here), but verses 3–7 of the chapter introduce the main subject of the story, namely Joseph and Mary and the birth of their child.

At the start of chapter 3 Luke employs the same trick yet again. One could hardly better this (not, at any rate, in the New Testament) for solemnity:

> In the fifteenth year of the *imperium* of Tiberius Augustus, when Pontius Pilate had *imperium* over Judaea, and Herod was tetrarch of Galilee, while Philip his brother was tetrarch of Iturea and the Trachonite region, and Lysanias was tetrarch of Abilene, in the high priesthood of Annas and Caiaphas....

Now you might pause, as you hear this impressive sounding list, to reflect that it contains a rather unsavory group of characters. Reading on, however, you discover that these are not the focus of Luke's narrative. The person he is *really* interested in is John the Baptist, Zachariah's son, who is the recipient of the Word of God in the desert and who does the remarkable things outlined in the following seventeen verses. Once again, we are reminded that the gospel must be read attentively, as things may well not be what they seem. There is another example of this in the next chapter (4:18–21), where Jesus unexpectedly turns a quotation from Isaiah into an account of his whole ministry in terms of good news for the poor, liberty to captives, sight to the blind and so on. This is clearly an instruction about how we are to read the whole gospel. It may seem at first sight like an account of the doings of important people like emperors, governors and high priests, but in fact it tells of what God is doing for the poor and underprivileged, including the women.

One should read Luke with a sensitivity to what he is about. He is surely sending a signal of some sort when he places right at the beginning two independent-minded and unusual women, namely Elisabeth and her kinswoman Mary, so that whatever is read in the rest of the gospel is understood in the light of what these two have said and done. In particular, notice that the most important message in the whole gospel was given to Mary, as we are about to see.

A) THE ANNUNCIATION (1:26–38)

The first text that we shall look at is the annunciation to Mary.

In the sixth month, the angel Gabriel was sent from God to a city of Galilee whose name was Nazareth, to a virgin betrothed to a man whose name was Joseph of the house of David. And the virgin's name was Mariam.

The name of Mary is only conceded at the end of the sentence; but it is she who matters to Luke, and she whose consent is required. Two verses later we hear the angel's second utterance, which makes clear what is always important to remember in Luke's gospel, that God is in charge: "Do not be afraid, Mariam, for you have found a gift from God." The activity of God is the principal focus of Luke's interest in these two volumes.

The text continues, in response to Mary's calm question about how all this can be:

The Holy Spirit will come upon you, and the power of the Highest will overshadow you. And, look, Elisabeth your kinswoman, even she has conceived a son, in her old age, and this is the sixth month for her who was nicknamed "Barren." Because where God is concerned, nothing at all is impossible. And Mariam said, "Look–

God's slave woman: let it happen to me according to what you have said."

This is an important text. Mary is presented as a "slave woman," but the gospel presents her choice as freely made, so it is not as if she is thereby derogated. More important for Luke is that everyone, men and women, is invited to discipleship, to the holiness of being able to say "whatever God wants," not because they are told to do so, but because God is the only reality that matters.

B) THE VISITATION (LUKE 1:39–56)

Mary now goes off into the mountain country to see her elderly kinswoman who is so improbably pregnant, and Luke presents their meeting as a great occasion of the outpouring of the Holy Spirit. The Spirit enables Elisabeth to make the prophetic remark: "Blessed are you among women, and blessed is the fruit of your womb." These two women are the most important characters whom we have encountered so far. Not only are they the mothers of John and Jesus, but they have modeled how disciples should respond to God's invitation. We would be unfaithful to Luke's intentions were we to forget them in the chapters that follow.

Particular attention should be paid to the remarkable hymn that Luke places on Mary's lips, which relativizes the political constructs of all human society:

My soul praises the greatness of the Lord and
My spirit has rejoiced over God my Savior,
Because he has looked on the low status of his slave woman
For, look, from now on all generations will congratulate me
Because The Powerful One has done great things for me
And holy is God's name.
And God's mercy is forever for those who revere God.
God's power has done a mighty deed,
Scattered those who are intellectually arrogant in their hearts.
God has torn down officials from [their] thrones,

The rich, God has sent away empty.
God has looked on the child Israel, to remember about mercy.
As God told our ancestors, Abraham and his descendants for all time.

This is not the utterance of a woman who is interested in quiet submission to patriarchy. The term "slave woman" is relativized by the introduction of God's astonishing power, and her "low status" is in relation to God, not man. This is an assertion that things are not the way they ought to be, and that God is going to make some changes.

c) THE BIRTH AND NAMING OF JOHN THE BAPTIST (LUKE 1:57–62)

Something similar is visible in this next scene, in which an independent-minded mother is vindicated:

> Meanwhile, Elisabeth's time was fulfilled for her to give birth: and she produced a son. And the neighbors heard, and her kinsfolk, that God had been very compassionate on her; and they came to rejoice with her. And it came to pass on the eighth day, they all came to circumcise the child. And they were all set to call him by his father's name, Zachariah. And his mother responded and said "NO! He is going to be called John." And they told her "No one of your tribe has been known by that name." And they tried to make signs to the child's father about what he wanted it to be called....

The boy was indeed called John and grew up with the name of the Baptizer or Baptist, and it was his mother's intervention that made it possible.

d) SYMEON AND HANNA (2:34–38)

Next we encounter Symeon, who addresses his prophecy to Mary, rather than Joseph.

> And Symeon blessed [Jesus' father and mother] and he said to Mariam, Jesus' mother: "Look, this one is set for the fall and rise of many in Israel, and for a sign that is opposed. And as for your

own life—a sword will pass through it, so that the doubts of many hearts may be revealed."

It is Mary whom Luke regards as important here, and the message is given added emphasis by the introduction of yet another woman:

> And there was Hanna, a prophet, a daughter of Phanuel, of the tribe of Asher: she was advanced in many days, living with her husband seven years after her bath-mitzvah, and she was a widow of as many as eighty-four years. She never left the Temple, with fasting and praying, offering her liturgy night and day. And at that hour she gave thanks to God, and spoke about God [or: about Jesus] to all those who were waiting for the redeeming of Israel.

This woman is a prophet ("prophetess" is what Luke actually wrote) who exercises her ministry publicly in the Temple, and in fact reaches a wider audience with her remarks than did Symeon, who spoke only to the parents of Jesus. Once again, Luke lets us see a woman speaking God's word into the situation.

e) THE DISAPPEARANCE AND REDISCOVERY OF JESUS (2:48–51)

Our next text has Jesus in the Temple with the teachers. Notice how little respect those teachers get from the worried mother, who erupts into the adolescent's theological discussion:

> And when [Jesus' parents] saw him, they were greatly astounded. And his mother said to him, "Child, why did you treat us like this? Look, your father and I have been terribly worried looking for you." And he said to them, "Why on earth where you looking for me? Didn't you realize that I would inevitably be at my Father's place?" And they did not grasp the word he spoke to them. And he went down with them and came to Nazareth, and was *subordinated* to them. And his mother kept these things in her heart.

Several things about this episode should be noted. First, the mother is not portrayed as demure and submissive; she takes the initiative in reproaching the boy for his lack of thought. Second, although he responds with a reproach, it is the mother who is in the right. As the story is told, it was a thoughtless act by the young man. Third, Jesus is revealed as under the authority of his parents, even if he has restated the identity of his Father as being other than Joseph. Finally, the episode is incomplete. The full significance of Jesus has not yet been made clear, a fact indicated by the meditative stance that his mother adopts as she "kept all these things in her heart."

f) THE WOMAN WHO ANOINTED JESUS (7:36–50)

Our next text is from Luke's account of one of a series of dinner parties that go disastrously wrong:

> One of the Pharisees invited him to eat with him, and he went into the house of the Pharisee and lay down to eat. And look: a woman who was a sinner in the city, and who knew that he was lying down in the house, brought an alabaster jar of myrrh. And standing behind, by his feet, she wept; and with her tears she started to wet his feet and with the hair of her head she wiped and kissed his feet and anointed them with myrrh.
>
> The Pharisee who had invited him saw this and said to himself, "If this chap were a prophet, he would know who she is, and of what class of person, this woman that's touching him. He would know that she is a sinner." And Jesus responded and said to him: "Simon, I have something to say to you." So he said, "Teacher, speak." "There were two debtors to a certain creditor. One owed five hundred denarii, and the other owed fifty. They had no way of repaying, and he let them both off. So which of them will love him more?" Simon answered and said, "I suppose the one who had more let off." Jesus said to him, "You have given the correct verdict."
>
> And he turned to the woman and said to Simon, "You see this woman? I came into your house, but you did not give me water for my feet, whereas she with her tears wet my feet; and with her hair she wiped them. You did not greet me with a kiss, whereas she ever since I came in has not ceased hugging and kissing my feet. You did not anoint my head with olive oil, whereas she anointed

my feet with myrrh. Because of this, I tell you, her sins, many sins, are forgiven, because she loved much. The person who doesn't have much forgiven, doesn't love much." And he said to her, "Your sins are forgiven you." And those who lay down said among themselves, "Who is this who even forgives sins?" He said to the woman, "Your faith has saved you—go in peace."

This passage has elicited much discussion from feminist scholars. In the other three gospels the story of a woman anointing Jesus is placed at the beginning of the passion narrative. Mark, whose account Luke presumably knew, has apparently inserted it there, in order, as we have already seen, to shed light on the passion, which is about to happen. Some scholars chide Luke for taking the story out of this context in the passion, wherein Mark, Matthew and John agree that it was a woman who anointed Jesus as Messiah. Instead, Luke has reduced the woman to a "sinner." But consider the following points: first, Luke's is a gospel of forgiveness and repentance, and what he has done here is to refashion the story, not in order to keep women in their place, but to give a dramatic description of what repentance and forgiveness look like.

Second, the woman is not a decorative addition to patriarchal domesticity, but a rather disturbing force in the household. She takes the initiative in upsetting the dinner party and starts off, very disturbingly, by *weeping*.

Third, though she is described as a "sinner," and male exegetes have often seized on this and characterized her as "a prostitute," she is undoubtedly the hero of the narrative. She has our attention from the beginning and is triumphantly vindicated at the end, though she says not a single word. If she is a sinner, she is not exceptional in that respect.

Fourth, the woman *is* exceptional in another respect: she shows great love. Jesus points to this by asking Simon the apparently irrelevant question about the two debtors. The point is that it is not really the person who has been forgiven most who loves most; it is rather that love brings with it an awareness of our need for forgiveness. The woman's tears and her loving actions reveal not that she has been a great sinner, but that she gives an absolute priority to love.

Finally, the woman is clearly commended over Simon. Her extravagant expression of love contrasts with the chilly neglect that Simon's politeness has failed to conceal. The final words that Jesus speaks, "Your sins are forgiven you....Your faith has saved you; go in peace," are beautiful. They are close to the heart of the mystery of humanity, and close too, therefore, to the mystery of divinity, but they are words that Simon cannot really hear because he does not realize his need of them. It is the woman who is vindicated in this story because her actions are a clarion call that speak far louder than words.

G) LUKE'S "PICNIC" (8:1-3)

Immediately following this episode, and not to be too radically separated from it, is another passage that has aroused a good deal of comment, not all of it favorable to the evangelist (8:1-3):

> And it happened immediately afterwards that he was traveling through, by city and village, announcing and giving the victory tidings of the reign of God, and the Twelve with him, and certain women who had been cured of wicked and unclean spirits, Mary called Magdalene, from whom seven demons had gone out, and Joanna the wife of Houza, Herod's foreman, and Susanna, and many others who used to minister to him [or: to them] from their possessions.

This passage emphasizes the importance of the women in the early community and implicitly admits the leadership of Mary Magdalene, who then disappears without trace in the second volume of this work. On the other hand, the women clearly have a different function from that of the Twelve. They are people with resources and possibly also a certain social status, but who are not, however, part of the *real* discipleship, for real discipleship is itinerant and radically poor. There is also the matter that these women have been cured of various unpleasant spirits, while the men are not said to have been cured of anything in particular, unless you go all the way back to the call of Peter at 5:8. And, lastly, Luke uses the word *diakoneo* to describe the women's activity, which I have translated as "minister to." It is connected, of course, with the English word *deacon* and denotes a function in the early church. We shall see, for example, that it is used with regard to Phoebe at Romans 16:1. Here, however, the function is reduced to that of organizing the "picnic," a phenomenon that we shall also observe in the next passage. Some feminists fear that Luke's agenda here is to make it quite clear that, although women have a function of some sort in the church, they are not on the same level as the men, and they must not get ideas above their station.

H) DINNER WITH MARTHA AND MARY (10:38–42)

Our next episode is the story of another dinner party, that of Martha and Mary.

> While they were on the journey, he went into a certain village; now a certain woman, Martha by name, received him. And she had a sister called Mariam, who sat at the Lord's feet and was listening to his word. Meanwhile Martha was dragged here and there with much *diakonia*. She stood and said, "Lord, don't you care that my sister has left me to *deacon* alone? Tell her to help me." And Jesus said, "Martha, Martha, you are concerned and anxious about many things, but only one is needed. For Mariam has chosen the good portion, which shall not be taken away from her."

This passage has caused a certain amount of ill-feeling. Many of us, certainly anyone who has seen a sibling or spouse or fellow member of the community not playing their part, instinctively sympathize with Martha and feel that she may have been the loser here. In addition, some feminists point out that the two words that I have italicized and translated as *diakonia* and *deacon* respectively are here being used quite clearly to refer to domestic tasks, as though they had no technical hierarchical significance in the early church. They argue that, once again, Luke is trying to keep women in traditional roles.

These thinkers also rule out another move that has been made in recent years by Christians anxious to rescue Jesus as a feminist and the gospel of Luke as pro-women. While some have emphasized that, in his Jewish context, Jesus was showing remarkable liberality in dealing so freely with women and taking them seriously as persons with whom to talk about the things of God, many feminists take a different perspective. They argue that this downgrades Jesus' Jewish background, not only because of its covert anti-Judaism, but also because recent studies indicate that first-century Judaism may have been more open to women than we have tended to suppose. This means that Jesus' openness to women, which cannot be denied, may not particularly distinguish him from other Jews. Additionally, they point out that here, unlike in John chapter 4, nobody seems particularly surprised that Jesus is talking so openly to women about the things of God.

We notice, first, that it is part of the great journey of Luke-Acts. The idea of "journeying" is absolutely central to Luke's grasp of the gospel and to his understanding of who Jesus is. "Journeying" also requires, however, the notion of stages on the journey, and this is one such stage. It does not follow that women must never move; it does follow that the gospel requires not only itinerant preachers but also stable house-churches, such as the one that Jesus visits here. So we are meant to approve the fact that Martha exercises the necessary charism of hospitality.

Mary is the subordinate sister; it is Martha who does the receiving while Mary "sits at his feet." However, Mary is *also* approved, for it is clearly proper for a disciple to "sit at the feet of the Lord" and to "hear the word of the Lord." On the other hand, *diakonia* is also a good thing to be doing, along with the addressing of Jesus as *Kyrie* or "Lord," as Martha does in verse 40.

Undeniably, however, there is a shock in the story—not because Martha was so outspoken, but because she is "pulled here and there" or "distracted," which leads her into a tone of voice that is presumably inappropriate for a disciple. On the other hand, Jesus' rebuke, with the reiteration of her name, is very gentle and springs from a desire for her not to be needlessly worried. It may indeed be no more than a request that she not prepare anything very elaborate, for "only one [dish?] is needed." We are not obliged to feel that Jesus must have disparaged one or the other.

Mine is not the only way of reading this passage, but at least we can argue that the passage is rich in ways that are not so obvious if only read through the feminist "lens" with its "hermeneutics of suspicion."

1) TWO WOMEN'S PARABLES (13:20–21 AND 15:8–10)

The next passage shows a sharp eye for woman's work. It is the lovely, all too brief, parable of the yeast:

> And again he said, "To what shall I compare the reign of God? It is like yeast, which a woman took and hid in three vats of wheat flour until the whole lot was leavened."

This is a daring and heartening parable, for God, it says, is like a woman, working quietly but powerfully. The same esteem for "women's work" is also evident in the second parable:

> Or what woman who has ten drachmae, if she loses one drachma does not kindle a lamp and sweep the house and look carefully for it until she finds it? And when she finds it, she calls her girlfriends and neighbors saying "Rejoice with me, because I have found the drachma which I have lost." So, I tell you, there is joy among the angels over one sinner repenting.

Once again, we see, God is compared to a woman; the author of this parable (Jesus or Luke; perhaps both Jesus *and* Luke) has a sharp eye for the ordinary things of domestic life. The drachma is a tiny sum, and many women will echo the experience of not having enough to manage the house on. And to compare the experience of losing and rediscovering one's precious hoard to the experience of God is daring and touching. God, it turns out, knows from experience the sadness and joy of women's lives.

The translation here endeavors to bring out the fact that the celebration party is more of a woman's event, and that God and Jesus understand the stresses to which a woman's life is susceptible.

j) THE POOR WIDOW'S CONTRIBUTION (21:1–4)

Our next passage carries something of the same message:

> He looked up and saw the men who were putting their gifts into the offering box; and they were rich. Then he saw a certain poor widow putting two small coins there. And he said, "I'm telling you, that poor widow put in more than the others. For all those men gave from their surplus into the offertory, but she from her lack put in all the means of sustenance that she had."

In the verse immediately preceding these (20:47), Luke has Jesus criticize the scribes precisely on the grounds that they combine "devouring the houses of widows" with "long hours of make-believe prayer." So the gospel is well aware of the hardships that religious authorities can impose on the economically helpless, especially women. Luke's gospel, however, *also* wants to say that it is possible to trust in God and that having enough to live on is *relatively* unimportant. One might argue that he would be better off saying this about the scribes than about the widow, who presumably already knew this only too well. The constant thrust of Luke's gospel is that the marginalized are not marginalized in God's eyes, nor incapable of being true disciples. Certainly it cannot be denied that here a widow woman is singled out as having done something greatly superior to the wealthier and presumably religiously orthodox men.

k) MALE AND FEMALE DISCIPLES ON THE WAY TO THE CROSS (23:26–29)

Our next passage appears only in Luke and comes as Jesus is making his final journey to "Skull Place":

> And as they were leading him out, they got hold of one Simon, a Cyrenean, coming from the field, and put the cross on him to carry it after Jesus. There followed him a great crowd of the people, and of women who were mourning and lamenting for him. Jesus turned to them and said to them, "Daughters of

Jerusalem, don't weep over me. Instead, weep for yourselves and for your children, for look, days are coming when people will say 'Happy are the women who are barren, and the wombs that have not given birth and breasts that have not suckled....'"

The African Simon is a disciple, doing just what disciples are supposed to do, according to this gospel (9:23). The women are also disciples, and here Luke uses of them the technical term which I have translated as "followed." They are part of the "great crowd of the people," like those who were waiting for Zachariah (1:10); and the most interesting segment of them is definitely the women. The Greek makes it clear that it was they alone who were lamenting Jesus' imminent death.

L) MALE AND FEMALE DISCIPLES AT THE CROSS (23:49)

Our next passage (23:49) is after Jesus' death, and reads, in Luke's version:

All the men known to Jesus stood there, looking from afar, and also women who had followed him from Galilee. The women were watching these things.

You may find it interesting to compare this with what is found in Mark's gospel (Mark 15:40). For Mark the only followers of Jesus who were present at the crucifixion were the women, but Luke has added "Jesus' acquaintances." I have translated them as "men" because that is the grammatical form of the Greek, and although the masculine form can operate inclusively, if the evangelist then goes on to mention the women (resuming contact with Mark) he presumably intends some kind of distinction between the men and the women. It is hard to tell who these "acquaintances" are supposed to be, but it may be intended as some kind of defense of the men against the charge of having abandoned Jesus.

M) FEMALE DISCIPLES AT THE TOMB (23:55–24:11)

Our next passage is the last view of women that the gospel gives us. As we read it, we shall do well to remember our first view of Mary and Elisabeth, which opened the gospel:

> Now the women who had followed on behind, the ones who had come with him from Galilee, saw the tomb and how the body was disposed. They went back and prepared perfumes and myrrh. And during the Sabbath, they rested in accordance with the commandment.
>
> But on the Sunday, in the deep dawn, they came to the tomb bringing the perfumes they had prepared. But they found the stone rolled away from the tomb; when they went in, they did not find the body of the Lord Jesus. And as they were wondering if they had the right place, look, two men stood near in glistening clothing. The women became fearful and bowed their faces to the ground; the men said to them, "Why are you looking for the Living One along with the corpses? He is not here; instead, he has risen. Remember how he spoke to you while he was still in Galilee saying that 'the Son of Man will inevitably be handed over into the hands of men who are sinners and be crucified and on the third day rise up?'" And they remembered his words.
>
> And they returned from the tomb and announced all these things to the eleven and to all the rest of the men. And they were the Magdalene Mary and Joanna and Mary of Jacob and the rest of the women with them. They said these things to the apostles and these words appeared before them as pure nonsense. And they did not believe the women.

It is sometimes argued that Luke has here changed what Mark wrote in order to put the women in a negative light, for they are not believed by the apostles or the other men. The women are rebuked by the angels and reveal their subordination to the two "men" by bowing their faces to the ground. On the other hand, what is one to do when faced with an apparition of that sort?

Furthermore, the women were correct in what they said: the tomb *was* empty, and Jesus *had* risen, and there is no suggestion that the "two men in glistening clothing" were hallucinations. The women seem, moreover, to have been present in fairly large numbers, to judge by the way the list is presented. So there is a good deal to be said in their favor. It is true that the angel implies that they should have remembered Jesus' words in Galilee, but since there are no words like this in the whole of the gospel, they might be pardoned for their forgetfulness.

The men were not merely unduly skeptical but also acted somewhat cowardly. Luke says that it was women, led by Mary Magdalen, who were apostles to the apostles and who brought to the men the news that Jesus was indeed risen.

2. ACTS OF THE APOSTLES

As in Luke, so in Acts a good many women are named, though they are far fewer than the men whose names are given. They tend to be wealthy (see, for example, 13:50; 17:4, 12, 34), the post-Easter equivalents, perhaps, of the "picnic ladies" of Luke 8:1–3. Women are certainly in the groups that compose the infant church (see 1:9–14; 5:14; 21:5), and Saul is clearly stated as having hunted down both men and women (8:3; 9:2; 22:4). Generally only the men are addressed (1:16), and there is no question that Judas might be replaced as an apostle by a woman (1:21-26). The women are there, with the odd exception of Mary Magdalen, but not in any position of leadership. What was Luke doing? Was he suppressing evidence of women's leadership or reflecting the situation of his own day, or did he simply have no indication that women had positions of authority in the church of which he is writing? For our look at Acts, we shall simply look at the five principal episodes that depict women and see what they can tell us.

a) ANANIAS AND SAPPHIRA (5:1-11)

A certain man called Ananias, along with Sapphira his wife, sold a property and embezzled some of the price with his wife's complicity; and he brought part of the sum and laid it at the feet of the apostles. Peter said, "Ananias, why did Satan fill your heart for you to cheat the Holy Spirit and embezzle part of the price of the field? If it had stayed with you it would have remained yours, and when sold, it would have been under your control. Why did you plot this deed? You were cheating God, not human beings." Ananias heard these words, fell down and expired; and great fear came on all who heard of it. The younger men got up, removed him, took him out and buried him.

There was an interval of about three hours, and his wife, who had no idea of what had gone on, came in. Peter greeted her with "Tell me, was such-and-such the price for which you sold the field?" She said, "Yes, such-and-such." Peter said to her, "Why did the two of you agree to tempt the Spirit of the Lord? Look—the feet of those who buried your husband are at the door, and they will carry you out." Instantly she fell down at his feet and expired. The young men came in and found her dead and carried her out and buried her next to her husband. And a great fear came on the whole church and on all who heard these things.

This is a very stylized narrative: the repetition of "at the feet" picks up the verse just before the start of the story, where it was said in the context of praise for the "communism" of the early church, that "all those who owned land or houses sold them and brought the proceeds and laid them at the feet of the apostles." Then there are the young men who know exactly what to do and removed the corpses one after another. There is also the fact that Sapphira comes at just the right time, when there has been no apparent attempt to contact her about her husband's funeral arrangements. Lastly, there is no trial or interrogation nor any endeavor to establish the truth of what has happened. I am of the opinion that what we have here is simply a grimly comic legend. It is not meant to be taken seriously, but is simply a dramatic presentation of the main thrust of Acts—that you cannot cheat the Holy Spirit.

B) TABITHA (9:36–43)

In Joppa there was a certain woman-disciple called Tabitha, which can be translated as Dorcas. She was full of good works and of almsgiving. Now it happened in those days that she fell sick and died. So they washed her and placed her in an upstairs room. Now Lydda was near Joppa, and the disciples, hearing that Peter was there, sent two men to him, urging him "Don't hesitate to come as far as us." Peter rose up and went with them. When he got there, they took him to the upper room, and all the widows stood before him weeping and showing him tunics and garments which Dorcas had made while she was still with them. Peter threw them all out; then he knelt down and prayed, and turned towards the corpse and said: "Tabitha, arise." She opened her eyes, and, seeing Peter, sat up. He gave her his hand and raised her up, and he called the [male?] saints and the widows and gave her back to them alive. It became known throughout the whole of Joppa, and many people believed in the Lord. It came to pass that he stayed a good few days in Joppa with Simon the Tanner.

Like Jesus before him (Lk 7:11–17), Peter raises a widow from the dead. It is pointed out by critics that (1) Tabitha is not allowed any status in the church, and (2) it was two *men* who were sent to Lydda to find Peter. That may, of course, simply reflect the church that Luke knew: for our evangelist, the function of this story is fairly clearly to establish the status of Peter, not over women or anyone else in the church, but as one who is continuing the Spirit-filled work of Jesus. Once again, this story has the air of a legend, as for example in the line "it happened in those days that she fell sick and died." This does not mean, necessarily, that it did not happen, but stresses the fact that Luke tells the story for reasons outside the story itself.

C) RHODA AT THE GATE (12:11–17)

And Peter came to himself and said, "Now I know for sure that the Lord has sent his messenger and has rescued me from the hand of Herod, and from all the expectation of the people of the Jews."

And when he understood, he went to the house of Mary the mother of John who is surnamed Mark, where a good few were gathered together and praying. When he knocked on the door of the entrance gate a slave girl called Rhoda approached to answer the door and recognizing Peter's voice, because of her joy, didn't open the main gate, but ran off and said that Peter was standing at the entrance. They said to her "You're crazy." She, however, insisted that it was so. And they said, "It's his guardian angel." Meanwhile Peter kept on knocking at the door; they eventually opened, and saw him, and they were struck all of a heap. He held up his hand to quiet them, and explained to them how the Lord had brought him out of prison and said, "Tell this to James and the brethren." And he went out and journeyed to another place.

This is clearly another story about Peter, and, as with the story of Ananias and Sapphira, I feel certain that there are comic elements. As in the case of the disciples after the resurrection (Luke 24:41), it was joy that caused Rhoda's odd behavior. Some scholars think that Rhoda was dismissed as crazy because she was both a slave and a woman; that may be so, but what would *they* have said if Rhoda had brought this report to them? And, in any case, the fact is that she was right, and her hearers remarkably wrong, and indeed substituted a less probable explanation ("It's his guardian angel") in their attempt to avoid the truth. Incidentally, the reader may observe that Mary is a church mother there in Jerusalem, for it is apparently her house to which Peter repairs.

d) THE WOMEN AT PHILIPPI (16:11–40)

And setting sail from Troas we sailed straight to Samothrace, and on the next day to Nea Polis, and from there to Philippi, which is the first city of the district of Macedonia, a colony. We stayed some days in this city. And on the Sabbath day we went out of the gate down by a river, where we thought there was a prayer-place, and we sat down and spoke with the women who came together.

And one woman, called Lydia, a dealer in purple cloth from the city of Thyateira, a woman who worshiped God, heard this; and the Lord opened her heart to pay attention to the things said by Paul. And when she was baptized, she and all her house, she invited him saying, "If you have decided that I am a believer in the Lord, come and stay, all of you, in my house," and she urged us.

Now it happened as we were journeying to the prayer-place that a certain slave girl who had a spirit of divination came out against us. She had produced a fair profit for her masters by prophesying. She followed Paul and shouted out at us saying, "These people are slaves of God the Most High, who are proclaiming to you the way of salvation." She did this for several days. Paul got fed up, turned round, and said to the spirit, "I command you in the name of Jesus Christ to come out of her." And it came out of her at that hour....{There follows an account of the imprisonment of Paul and Silas and their escape}...and coming out of prison they went to Lydia's, and they saw the Christians and comforted them and went out.

In this interesting passage we meet Lydia, a worker in the purple-dye trade. Since that is a luxury item and since she evidently had a substantial household, of which she was clearly in charge, one assumes that she was well-to-do. Some scholars argue that Lydia was fighting with Paul for the right to be taken seriously as a Christian, although that seems unlikely at this stage of her conversion. Perhaps the most interesting of all is the fact that Paul went to what appears to have been a "woman's synagogue" by the river and made converts there, which at least argues for the openness of Jewish women to his message.

E) PRISCILLA AND AQUILA (18:1-4, 18-19, 24-28)

After this he departed from Athens and came to Corinth, and finding a certain Jew called Aquila, who was Pontic in origin and had recently come from Italy, and Priscilla his wife, because of Claudius having decreed that all Jews were to depart from Rome, he came to them because they were of the same trade; and he worked—for they were tent makers by trade. And he would debate in the synagogue every Sabbath, and persuade both Jews and Greeks...

Paul, having stayed a decent number of days, said good-bye to the Christians and sailed out to Syria. With him were Priscilla and Aquila, who cut his hair at Cenchreae, for he had a vow. And they got to Ephesus, and left them there while he went into the synagogue and debated with the Jews....

Now a certain Jew called Apollos, of Alexandrian origin, an eloquent man, came to Ephesus, very strong on the Scriptures. He was instructed in the way of the Lord, and spoke with spiritual enthusiasm, and taught accurately the things about Jesus; but he only knew John's baptism. He began to speak fearlessly in the synagogue, and when Priscilla and Aquila heard him they got hold of him and explained the way more accurately for him.

We shall come across this couple when we look at St. Paul, and there we shall see that the order of their names sometimes varies, but that normally Priscilla comes first (as she does here on two out of the three occasions where they are named). This suggests that she was the more significant figure and that it was she who catechized the distinguished intellectual Apollos. There is no indication here that Priscilla is in any way classed as an inferior, and indeed her leadership seems to be implicitly conceded in these verses.

After reviewing all these passages in Acts, it is clear that there *were* women in the church who were known to Luke. He does not appear to have felt that they had leadership functions, though he does not precisely deny such a function with regard to Lydia and Priscilla. It is interesting to note that at 6:1–6 a problem between the widows of two racial groups is solved, not by the women themselves, but by the appointment of six unambiguously male deacons, and feminist scholars also point to Luke's slightly offhand treatment of Philip's prophet-daughters at 21:9 as evidence that he was determined to exclude any hint of a serious role for women. This may only reflect the world that he knew and that he found in his sources.

Conclusion

What, then, at the end of this long chapter, can we say of the way in which Luke handles the evidence for women in the church? Certainly, we have seen reason to doubt the older view, that Luke was friendly to women *simply* because he mentioned so many of them. Mary Magdalen disappears completely from Luke's church (and from the whole of the New Testament after the gospels) as soon as she has performed her last function of witnessing to the resurrection. And there is something of a takeover by the males as the first volume gives way to the second. On the other hand, as we have seen, Acts does not deny that women had significant roles in the church, and, in particular, that many were great followers of Paul's and that he was enormously assisted by them. We should note, furthermore, the way in which the whole gospel begins, the signals that Luke gives us that the most important people are not necessarily those whom you would expect. Thus, we need to look again at his portrayal of women and see them all bathed in the light of those powerful and striking figures with whom the story begins: of Mary and Elisabeth and Hanna the prophet. Even if Luke did not intend it so, their powerful presence at the beginning of the story should inform the way we read the whole of these two volumes. Mary, who gave a slightly puzzled "Yes" to the angel, Elisabeth who recognized the mother of her Lord, and Hannah, who spoke about the child to all who were awaiting the redemption of Israel, are heroes of the narrative. They serve as models for the reader to imitate and sources of profound encouragement for us all.

CHAPTER EIGHT

WAS IT ALL THE FAULT OF PAUL?

IN THIS CHAPTER, WE SHALL BE LOOKING AT one of the most original thinkers of the early church and one of the most influential characters in Christian history, at whose door some feminists lay almost all the blame for Christian prejudice against women. In asking about Paul's views on women, however, it could be argued that we are raising a thoroughly inappropriate question, on the grounds that it is unreasonable to interrogate him about the eminently twentieth-century question of the status of women in his writings. We come to him with our own agenda and our own pressing problems, but we have also to respect what it was he was trying to do.

So far as it goes, there is something in this argument: an ancient author is necessarily a man or woman of their time, and we cannot very well ask them to be something else, with views on each of our modern problems, or we shall be inventing an author who never existed. Paul's primary focus was not on the status of women, but on what God has done in Jesus and how Christians are to proclaim that message in the contemporary world. On the other hand, it is reasonable for us to ask how Paul would handle the question. In Paul's case, moreover, there is the problem that texts written by him or, as we shall see in the next chapter, disseminated in his name, have been used to keep women in subservient roles. Some of his disciples presumably thought that they were being faithful to him when they tried to restrict the activities of women in the church, with results that are still with us today.

There are seven letters widely regarded by scholars as "authentic Paul," namely Romans, 1 and 2 Corinthians, Galatians, Philippians, 1 Thessalonians and Philemon. Scholars are divided on 2 Thessalonians, but that need not worry us. In fact, we shall restrict ourselves to selected portions of only five of these letters, namely Galatians, 1 Corinthians, Romans, Philippians and Philemon. In some ways it is a mistake to take such a narrow slice through Paul, for many scholars argue that one should take the whole Pauline corpus, even texts not apparently directly about women, and analyze them through one of the possible feminist "lenses."

A) GALATIANS 3:26–28

Galatians is Paul's most consistently "bad-tempered" letter. He is so cross that he conspicuously fails to do what he does in all his other letters—thank God for the virtues of the people to whom he is writing. The problem is that after Paul had preached the gospel to the Galatians, they started to believe something else. He had announced that faith in what God had done in Jesus was sufficient for them; then others had come and told them that in order to be a follower of Jesus a person had to accept the ordinary requirements of Judaism, namely circumcision, dietary laws and the feast days celebrated by Jews. And the Galatians had accepted all this even though Paul thought that he had made it clear to them that there were *no* conditions attached to the gospel. "You *stupid* Galatians," he rails at them, "who has bewitched you?" (3:1). So our passage comes as he is trying to explain to them that they have got it wrong, using arguments that are not always easy to follow and culminating, at the end of chapter 3, in the following sentences:

> For you are all children of God through faith in Christ Jesus. For given that you were baptized into Christ, you put on Christ, [like a cloak], and [in him] there is no such thing as Jew or Greek, no such thing as slave or free, no such thing as male and female. For you are all one in Christ Jesus. And if you belong to Christ, then you are descendants of Abraham, heirs according to the promise.

Now it is important to admit that I have to some extent cheated in this translation, for Paul wrote not "children of God," but "sons of God." In addition, the letter as a whole is clearly, if unconsciously, addressed to the males in Galatia, for he speaks often of circumcision

and calls his addressees "sons" and "brothers" as he does in all his
other letters. The passage I have quoted comes at the end of an argument where he described the Torah, the Jewish law, in terms of the
paidagogos or "tutor" assigned to a young man in a well-to-do Greek
household. Only a boy would be under the harsh supervision of this
disciplinarian, and indeed the argument is really dependent on the
idea of the *eldest* son. So we must be cautious about embracing this passage too enthusiastically as indicating conscious antipatriarchal and
feminist tendencies on Paul's part. Nevertheless, the implication of
this passage is clearly that the fundamental divisions between human
beings are relativized, once you have "put on Jesus" in baptism.

First, for those who are "in Christ," the ethnic and religious
divide between "Jew" and "Greek" is simply irrelevant, according to
Paul. We must not underestimate how radical a view this was in a
world acutely alive to national and, even more, religious boundaries.
The next phrase is still more radical, since it destabilizes one of the
economic and political pillars on which the prosperity of the
Roman empire was built, namely the distinction between "slave"
and "free." What about the third category? We have to move a little
more cautiously here. Feminists will point, with some justice, to the
fact that there were women (as well as men) who were Jewish and
Greek, and who were slaves and free, and they will ask if that
thought had crossed Paul's mind, suggesting that Paul rather for-
gets about the women in those categories. Paul writes "male **and**
female," whereas the other pairs are linked by "or." What is the difference? Here it seems that Paul must be referring to Genesis 1:27,
"Male and female God created them," and alluding to marriage.
The claim, therefore, is that in Christ Jesus you do not have to
observe Jewish law, and it no longer matters if you are a slave.
Baptism has canceled all that and made all the Galatian Christians
(and all the Christians all over the Mediterranean world) "one in
Christ Jesus." In the Christian community, therefore, women do not
need to be married in order to have status.

Here Paul is preaching, or rather, angrily reminding his readers
of the fact that he had preached, a gospel of freedom. Not long
afterwards he insists (5:1) that "it was for freedom that Christ freed

us; so stand firm and don't revert to putting your neck under the yoke of slavery." Jewish readers (and we must never forget that Paul was a Jew) will bridle at the description of the Law as "the yoke of slavery," nor will they care for the way in which Paul has handled the Hagar story in chapter 4, but Paul's concern is to defend the view that all those Christians, whatever their religious observance, are "brothers and sisters in Christ," for as the argument triumphantly concludes, "you are all one in Christ Jesus."

This baptismal formula undermines the principal social constructs of the world that Paul and his Galatians knew. He is trying to argue that being "in Christ Jesus" *made a difference.* And his expressing the claim in this way must have had the most extraordinary impact. Not only that, but it is possible to see here the first sketch of our modern view of the matter. This is a thoroughly radical doctrine whose full significance Paul certainly never had time to explore, but consider this: If slavery is irrelevant, then women slaves officially have status in this new world of being "in Christ." If baptism has replaced circumcision, then women as well as men are being addressed. And if marriage is not the only way in which women can find a role, then being unmarried is not somehow a failure. Indeed, in the world of that time Christianity may well have been the means of very great freedom for some women in that they no longer had to be some male's "significant other," but in and of themselves could have a role, for example as missionaries for the new group.

The logic of this baptismal formula—though Paul may not have seen all the way to the end of his logic—is that a new family is being formed from *all* walks of life (for if *these* divisions are seen as insignificant, then no other cultural divide could have any permanent status). It is a family that is defined only by being "in Christ Jesus." Therefore women and men are equal. In our century that may not seem a very odd thing to say, but in Paul's time it was social dynamite. It is small wonder if, as we shall be seeing, his lens did not always allow him to view reality in that way. Nor should we be too surprised or scandalized if some of his successors retreated, over the next generation or two, from this radical position.

B) 1 CORINTHIANS 11: 3-16

1 Corinthians is the letter that will get the most attention in this chapter. I shall not be attempting to give a detailed commentary on the letter, but simply point to certain passages relevant to our inquiry. Before we start, it may be worth noticing the view, based on the way in which the argument of the epistle is constructed, that the adversaries Paul has in mind throughout are a group of women prophets in Corinth who have challenged his authority in various ways.

Our first passage comes from chapter 11, where Paul is starting to consider questions about proper behavior in the liturgy. The particular question here is so remote from the presuppositions of our culture that without a copy of the letter that the Corinthians had sent to him it is very hard to have any confidence at all about what is at issue, except that it had something to do with heads, and women's heads at that. The argument goes in five stages:

Stage 1 (3-6): The Argument from Authority and Convention

> Now I want you to know that of every man Christ is the head, and the head of the woman is the man and the head of Christ is God. Every man who prays or prophesies with something on his head shames his head, whereas every woman who prays or prophesies with her head uncovered shames her head—for it is identical with having her head shaved. So if a woman is not covered, then let her be shorn; but if it is a disgrace for a woman to be shaved or shorn, let her be covered.

Living as we do at such a distance from the culture in which these words were written, we find it almost impossible to grasp what Paul is arguing here. Clearly the core of the argument concerns the "head," and Paul wants women's heads to be covered because in some way this represents the chain of authority which goes: God-Christ-Man-Woman. It is true that many scholars argue that "head" in this sense means "origin" rather than "authority," but I suspect that this does not make very much difference to the sense, which is that women are Other and that their garments must indicate as much. We may notice, though, that however this argument from convention works, Paul is quite clear that both men and women may be presumed to have identical roles in the liturgy of the Corinthian church, whether praying or prophesying.

Stage 2: The Argument from Scripture (7–9)

Paul now offers another argument, perhaps feeling that the previous one may not have won over all the Corinthians:

> For a man ought not to have his head covered, being the likeness and glory of God whereas the woman is the man's glory: for the man does not come from the woman, but the woman from the man. And moreover the man was not created on account of the woman, but the woman on account of the man.

While this may not seem utterly compelling to us, it is nevertheless possible that those who heard the letter read out in the Corinthian house-church were convinced by the argument. Every generation has its way of handling the Scriptures, which may appear simply unintelligible to another generation. The argument here is based on Scripture. When Paul argues that "man is the likeness and glory of God," he is alluding, perhaps a shade loosely, to Genesis 1:26–27, where the human race, both male and female, is created in God's image and likeness. When he speaks of the woman coming from the man, he is referring to the account in Genesis 2:22–23 of the creation of the woman from the man's rib. The view that the woman was created on the man's account comes from Genesis 2:18. It may be that Paul is dealing here with people who had not been brought up on the Torah and were therefore more readily impressed by arguments from Scripture than a group with a higher proportion of Jewish converts would have been, but the mere fact that we do not find the argument instantly decisive does not mean that they also did not. In any case, Paul evidently feels the need to draw another arrow from his quiver:

Stage 3: The Argument from the Angels (10)

> On this account the woman should have authority over her head,
> on account of the angels.

One could be forgiven for scratching one's head in astonishment
at the argument. There are various possible meanings. Some scholars point to that rather odd passage in Genesis 6:2, where the "sons
of God" fall in love with human women. If that is what Paul is thinking of, it would be a matter of the women having "authority" over
their heads in order to distract the angels' prurient gaze. This
"authority" was presumably in the form of some kind of head-dress,
which is why the word is often translated as "veil." An alternative
explanation comes from scholarly examination of the scrolls discovered half a century ago at Khirbet Qumran by the Dead Sea. Some
of those manuscripts, notably the "Scroll of the War of the Sons of
Light against the Sons of Darkness," strongly insist on the need for
ritual purity, including purity in sexual matters, on the grounds that
the angels are fighting alongside the human warriors. It may simply
be that Paul had a sense, in which presumably he expected the
Corinthian Christians to share, that the women had to be decent
because the angels somehow participated in their weekly liturgy.
Either way, the argument is not one that comes naturally to us.

Next there comes a pause in the argumentation, and Paul seems
to be hastily inserting a corrective, just in case he has somehow
implied that women are inferior to men:

Stage 4: Reciprocity between Men and Women (11–12)

> But of course in the Lord there is no such thing as the woman
> without the man, nor the man without the woman; for as the
> woman is out of the man, so the man comes through the woman.
> But the whole lot comes out of God.

Paul's position on the priority of the sexes certainly seems to be
that if anyone has the priority, it is God, and that men may not arro-
gate superiority to themselves. With that said, Paul now returns to

the argument, this time resting his case on what "nature herself teaches you":

Stage 5: Argument from Natural Law (13–15)

Judge among yourselves: do you think it appropriate for a woman to pray uncovered to God? Doesn't nature herself teach you, that if a man has long hair, it is a dishonor for him, whereas if a woman has long hair it is her glory? Because the long hair is given her as clothing.

Most societies today are familiar with women who have short hair and men whose hair is long, so that in most cultures this argument would be regarded as virtually unintelligible. Presumably it was not unintelligible in Corinth. As far as we can tell, in the ancient world women did wear their hair long, perhaps even long enough, as this text suggests, to use it as clothing. However, there were certainly Greek cultures where men had long hair, so perhaps the argument would not have been all that powerful even in Corinth. This may be the reason why the final stage of the argument seems more like a tirade than an exercise in reasoned dialogue:

Stage 6: Argument from Authority (16)

Now if anyone fancies being argumentative, we do not have such a custom.
And neither do the churches of God.

What are we to make of this? It looks as though Paul was uncomfortably aware that the reasoning he had employed so far may not carry absolute conviction and thus he resorts to the argument called "because I say so." Many of us who have been teachers have been driven to adopt this position late on a Friday afternoon, but Paul buttresses it with the rider that "everyone agrees with me." One of the overriding concerns of 1 Corinthians is church unity, both within the group at Corinth and in the church at large. The argument from the practice of other Christian groups is a perfectly reasonable one, but we should like to know how much conviction it carried with the Corinthians.

It is evident that Paul, for reasons about which we can no longer be perfectly clear, regards this question as one worth fighting for without being able to say precisely why it is important. Given the embarrassment he evidently feels about it and given what we know of the general atmosphere of Corinth, some scholars have suggested that perhaps his target was homosexual transvestitism, women dressing as men, and claiming in self-justification Paul's own "gospel of freedom." While that may be so, it cannot be demonstrated. Certainly, however, we have seen no reason here for the older Catholic practice that women had always to go to Church either veiled or wearing a hat. Still less is there anything in this passage that will enable us to say that Paul regarded women as inferior; and, finally, we have seen evidence that he assumed that they would play a full part in the liturgy.

Next we look at a passage that has frequently been used against women:

c) Silence in Church (14:34–36)

As in all the churches of the saints, let the women be silent in the churches. For it is not permitted for them to speak; but let them be *subordinated,* as even the Law says. And if they want to study anything, let them ask their own men at home. For it is disgraceful for a woman to speak in church. Or was it from you that God's word came out? Or did it come upon you alone [masculine]?

This is undeniably a tricky passage. It seems to contradict what we have already read in chapter 11 about women prophesying and praying in church, and it does not apparently fit well with Paul's assertion in Galatians. Many scholars argue, though not everyone concurs, that this passage does not fit well into the whole flow of chapters 12–14, and there is some disagreement in the manuscript tradition as to where these verses belong. Given all that, and, it must be said, given a certain embarrassment at the tone of what the author says here, some scholars have advanced the view that this was not written by Paul. They suggest that the tone here is more like that of the Pastoral Letters, which we shall be looking at in the next chapter: note the italicized word *"subordinated"* and the reference to women "learning," which in the next chapter we shall see reason to connect to the study of theology. The suggestion is that he did not write this passage, but rather that it was penned by someone else, perhaps the author of the Pastoral Letters, and was inserted into 1 Corinthians some time after Paul wrote it in order to claim Pauline authority for these repressive sentiments.

While that is possible, all the manuscripts agree in placing this passage somewhere towards the end of the letter, and it may simply have been the tone of the verses that led to its excision from some of the manuscripts. In any event, the fact remains that even if the passage is not from Paul's pen, Paul was thought to be a suitable mouthpiece for views of this sort. And, undeniably, some churchmen, and very conceivably some churchwomen also, held this opinion less than a century after the beginning of Christianity. Indeed some scholars, arguing that Paul did write this passage, suggest that he is making up his case as he goes along (we saw when we looked at chapter 11 that the argumentation there had a rather improvised feel to it), and only now feels strong enough to enjoin total silence on the women prophets at Corinth. Others, less astringently, say that it is only married women who are being silenced, simply to prevent disorder during the assembly. One odd fact is that the two questions at the end of the passage are apparently addressed, not just to the women, but to the Corinthians as a whole.

Whatever we may think of all this, it is not an easy text. Supposing that it came from the pen of St. Paul, does it follow, as we read it today, that fidelity to Scripture demands that women be quiet in church? It seems more likely that we should use our imagination and our historical skills to reconstruct the situation that Paul is dealing with and then ask ourselves what the appropriate response would be in our situation.

We have spent a good deal of time on 1 Corinthians because it seemed profitable to do so, but even so, we have not considered the oddities of chapter 7, the omission of the women witnesses to the resurrection in chapter 15 and the personal references to women in chapter 16. We can move on, however, reflecting that all that appears above the surface of the text is merely the tip of a fairly substantial iceberg, and if we are to draw conclusions from it about the appropriate treatment of women in the church of the twenty-first century, then we need a good deal more confidence about what was going on between Paul and his much loved, but undeniably combative, Corinthians.

d) ROMANS 16

Women are not specifically mentioned in the Letter to the Romans until we get to the final chapter. We may assume that they are included as members of the church at Rome whenever the text apparently addresses only the men, although we have to concede that Paul's focus may well have been primarily on the men. However, things are rather different in chapter 16, the parting commendations. Here there are manuscript difficulties, and not all codices are agreed that this part belongs with the rest of the letter. Whether or not it does, and I am inclined to suppose that it does, it is of particular interest given the subject matter:

> I commend to you our sister Phoebe, who is deacon of the church in Cenchreae, that you may give her in the Lord a welcome suitable for the saints, and may provide assistance for her in any matter where she has need of you. For she has been a patron of many, and of myself as well. Greet Prisca and Aquila, my coworkers in Christ Jesus, who put their own heads on the block to save my life; I am grateful to them—and it's not just me, but all the Gentile churches. And greet the church in their house....(16:1–5a)
> Greet Maria, who has worked hard for you. Greet Andronicus and Junia, my kinsfolk and fellow prisoners, who are conspicuous among the apostles, who were before me in Christ. (6–7)
> Greet Tryphaena and Tryphosa, workers in the Lord. Greet

Persis, the beloved lady, who has worked hard in the Lord. Greet
Rufus, the chosen in the Lord, and his mother and mine. (12–13)
Greet Philologus and Julia, Nereus and his sister. (15)

One third of the people greeted in these verses are women. The
fact that Paul salutes them in a letter in which he is trying to smooth
his path towards a church that he did not found and a group that he
is not personally acquainted with, suggests that the women mentioned in these verses were persons of some significance there.

The first mentioned is Phoebe, who is described as "our sister," a
key term in first-generation Christianity. It seems from the first two
verses that she may actually be carrying the letter. In addition, she is
described as "deacon of the church at Cenchreae." Cenchreae is the
easternmost of Corinth's two harbors and a place, therefore, of considerable importance, whose deacon will no doubt have been an
influential leader in the church. The translations often take the
option of translating the word as "deaconess," which reduces her
significance and which is not justified by the Greek. She is further
described by a word which means something like "patron" or
"chief" or "benefactress." So this woman, who is quite likely a traveling missionary, is a person of some importance in the church that
Paul knew.

So, too, is the next woman mentioned. Prisca, also referred to in
1 Corinthians 16 and Acts 18, is here described by Paul as a
"coworker," a title he gives later on in the chapter to Timothy (16:21;
cf. 1 Thes 3:2) and in 1 Corinthians to Apollos (1 Cor 3:9), as well as
others. For Paul, that is to say, Prisca is one of the most significant
Christian workers that he knew.

Lastly there is Junia (verse 7). Some translations, seeing that Paul
describes her (along with Andronicus, likely enough her husband)
as "my kinfolk, and fellow prisoners of mine, and well known
among the apostles," turn her into a man called Junias, on the
grounds that women simply cannot be apostles. This is not a complete invention, for the construction is grammatically possible.
There is no evidence, however, for holding that Junias was a man's
name, whereas Junia, named after Juno, queen of the gods, is well

attested as a woman's name. It is more likely that Paul, who knows no higher title for a Christian than that of "apostle," hailed her in these remarkable terms. Can we glimpse here a church that looks really rather different from the way we may have imagined the early church to be?

E) PHILIPPIANS 4:2–3

Before we leave Paul, I should like to look at two verses of Philippians, the most cheerful of Paul's letters. One has the feeling that it was with the church at Philippi, at the bottom end of Thrace in the northern Aegean, that Paul felt most at home. Even though he is writing from prison, he is evidently in close contact with them, for he is aware that there has been a dust-up of some sort. He writes (4:2–3):

> I encourage Evodia, and I encourage Syntyche, to think the same in the Lord. And I ask you, noble Syzygos, help these women, who have stood side by side with me in the gospel, along with Clement, and the rest of my fellow workers, whose names are in the book of life.

These are interesting verses from a number of points of view. Firstly, this "thinking the same" is what Paul was trying to urge on the Philippians as a whole when in chapter 2 of the letter he introduced that extraordinary hymn to Christ Jesus, "who being in the form of God, did not think equality with God a thing to be plundered...." It may be that the feud between these women was seriously dividing the group of Christians in Philippi, which would argue that they were persons of some influence there. Certainly the way that Paul refers to them would suggest as much, for he calls them "fellow workers" and we have seen above that this is strong language for Paul and a mark of high esteem. He also says of them that they "competed with me." I have translated that as "stood side by side" to avoid the implication, which is in English but not in Greek, that the two women were Paul's opponents. It is more like (indeed this is where the Greek word comes from) athletes on the same team, who have trained together, stood by each other, and who can expect to share the prize together.

And there is one other aspect of this passage, which I raise cautiously. As I have translated it, someone called "noble Syzygos" is asked to act as an intermediary in the tiff between Evodia and Syntyche. Now Syzygos is nowhere attested as a name; but it does have a meaning, namely "yoke-fellow," which could be a metaphor either for "fellow worker" or for "spouse." So I lay before you the possibility that far from being a misogynist celibate Paul may actually have been contentedly married and separated from his wife only by the demands of his apostolate. The evidence is, it must be said, both slim and circumstantial.

There is, first, the fact that Paul was a trained rabbi, and it was understood for obvious reasons that it was preferable for a rabbi to marry. Secondly, so far as we can tell, Paul's accusers never throw against him the charge of celibacy. Thirdly, in 1 Corinthians 9:5, 12, Paul claims forcefully that he has a perfect right "to take a Christian wife around with me," which would be an odd thing to say if it were known that no such wife existed. It is not much to go on, you may observe, but worth at least thinking about, for it makes a difference to how you read Paul.

What then to do with the frequent assumption that Paul himself was celibate? In fact, this depends on 1 Corinthians 7:7, 8 where Paul does not actually say that he is unmarried, nor does his argument require it. All that is required for the argument is that Paul is living a chaste life and that could be the case whether he is celibate, single, divorced, separated, widowed or away from his much-loved spouse in Philippi.

f) THE LETTER TO PHILEMON—A TAILPIECE TO ST. PAUL

Before finishing with this chapter, which in some ways is the most important of the whole book, simply because St. Paul gets blamed, not entirely without justice, for so much of the church's treatment of women, I want to have a brief look at the letter to Philemon (strictly speaking, to Philemon, Apphia, Archippus and the rest of their house-church). It must be a brief look, because it is only a brief letter, but of all the Pauline epistles it is the one that most resembles what we understand by a letter. It is worth pausing over since it touches on the issue of slavery, which we have seen to be related to the question with which this book deals. I shall take the letter paragraph by paragraph:

> Paul, a prisoner of Christ Jesus, and Timothy the brother, to Philemon the *beloved,* who is also our coworker, and to Apphia our sister and Archippus our fellow soldier, and to all the church in your house, grace to you and peace from God our father and the Lord Jesus Christ.

This is an entirely conventional opening to a letter by Paul. It would be possible to make a case for the view that Archippus is the one who is addressed (for the letter is couched in the second person singular, so it is not addressed to all of them). If, however, as is generally supposed, it was written to Philemon rather than Archippus, the first rather than the last to be mentioned, then we notice that the slave owner is described as beloved and as a coworker, both of which are terms of high praise in Paul's vocabulary. It is also possible that Paul is trying to establish Philemon's good will for the awkward request that he is going to make of him. We will also note, more germane to the inquiry that we are making in this book, that Apphia, who is clearly a woman, is of equal status with the other two.

The letter then continues:

> I give thanks to my God all the time, remembering you in my prayers, when I hear of your love and your faith which you have towards the Lord Jesus and to all the saints, so that the *communion* of your faith may become effective in the recognition of every good [person] among us into Christ. For I have had much joy and comfort in your love, because the saints have been given rest and repose in their inward parts through you, brother.

The translation may seem somewhat obscure, particularly the first sentence, but it gets across the gist of what he is about, and it must be said that the obscurity is in the Greek. Once again, notice how he uses the word "love," which I have italicized, as I have also the other key word, "communion." This translates the Greek word *koinonia,* which means things like partnership, fellowship, union and communion, and is a key word for Paul when he addresses the divisions of that squabbling church in Corinth as an expression for the quality of relationship that he thinks ought to exist between Christians who have broken bread together at the Lord's Supper. It is this attitude that Paul is asking Philemon to have toward all his fellow Christians, including those who happen to be runaway slaves. All church members, including slaves, are equal and equally deserving of love and fellowship. Twice in these lines Paul refers to the "saints," by which he means not those who are safely dead, but those who are alive, including those who have done wrong to us. Every word of this letter is carefully planned to leave Philemon in a rhetorical vice from which there is no escaping. The letter now continues:

> Therefore [although] I have much courage to command you [to do] what is fitting, I prefer to invite you [to do it] for *love's* sake, seeing as this is Paul, an old man now, and also a prisoner of Christ Jesus. I am inviting you with regard to my child, whom I have fathered here in prison, Profitable. He is the one who once upon a time was Useless, but has turned out to be Useful to you, and to me as well, and I am sending him to you, him, that is my "inward parts." I wanted to keep him by me, so that he might act as your agent, in being my deacon, here in the prison where the gospel has landed me; but I was reluctant to do anything without your permission, so that your good deed should be done by choice, and not under constraint.

Now Paul comes to the heart of the matter. The story is about a slave whose name is Onesimus, which in Greek means something like "profitable." Paul is clearly making a pun on that name, but he may also be making a rather sharp point at Philemon. Another pun comes in the terms that I have translated as "useful" and "useless." These are both connected with the word *chrestos,* fairly rare in most Greek writings, but surprisingly common in the New Testament. Reading it, I am reminded that it would almost certainly have been pronounced indiscernibly from the word *Christos* or "Christ." So Paul is not merely making a pleasant little joke on the name "Profitable," but also reminding Philemon that something has happened to Onesimus. This ambiguity in the words "useless" and "useful" is not easy to manage elegantly in English, but we perhaps express it best by saying that "the person who was once *Un*Christian is now *Good*Christian."

Paul, moreover, also calls Onesimus my "deacon," which does mean servant, but by this time in the church's history is also starting to take on the status of a technical term for a church official. Paul also refers to Onesimus as "my inward parts," significantly picking up a word he used earlier in his praise of Philemon for his service to fellow Christians.

In the next paragraph, he really gets down to business:

Perhaps this was the reason why he was temporarily removed from you, so that you might have him for eternity, no longer as a slave, but as something much higher than a slave, as a *beloved* brother. He is especially *beloved* to me; and I am sure that he will be much more so to you, both as a human being and as a fellow Christian [*literally:* both in the flesh and in the Lord]. So if you regard me as in *communion* with you, welcome him as though it were me. If he has done you an injury or owes you anything, charge it to my account. I, Paul, write with my own hand: I shall repay. I don't want to point out to you that you owe your whole self to me.

There is a hint of menace here; Paul is doing to Philemon what he also did to the Corinthians with regard to Timothy (1 Cor 16:10) and insisting that his emissary be received as though it were Paul himself, rather as in that world ambassadors actually stood for the monarch or country they represented. So Philemon has to receive his runaway slave as he would Paul! We may wonder whether he would have dared to do otherwise. Certainly he is being invited here to resolve a clash of values between his world, in which slaves must know their place and keep to it, and the world of the church, in which there is "no such thing as slave or free, Jew or Greek, male and female." Philemon is being invited to give proper expression to the *koinonia* or communion that he has with Paul. If it is anything at all, it must apply also to fellow Christians who are of a different race or a different gender, and to fellow Christians who are slaves, even if legally they are in the wrong.

Paul continues with something of a pun on Onesimus's name, and a reminder of the compliments with which he opened the letter:

> Yes indeed, my brother, I wish to gain Profit in the Lord. Give rest and recreation to my inward parts in Christ. I have written to you confident of your obedience, knowing that you will do more than what I say; and at the same time you can prepare a guest room for me. For I hope that through your prayers I shall cancel your debt. Epaphras my fellow prisoner greets you in Christ Jesus, as do Marcus, Aristarchus, Demas and Lukas, my fellow workers. The grace of Our Lord Jesus Christ be with the spirit of all of you.

This is a formidable letter, and it would be interesting to know more about the spirit in which Philemon received it. Paul is putting very considerable pressure on him. Some have even accused the apostle of shameful manipulation here. At any rate, it seems that perhaps it did the trick, for we know of a bishop called Onesimus (and it may be the same person) who was head of the church in Ephesus toward the end of the first century, and who made the collection of Paul's letters.

Nevertheless, some readers may have some questions for Paul. In the first place, given the penalties incurred by runaway slaves in the ancient world, Philemon must have been a fairly unpleasant master if Onesimus had the courage to flee from him, and to a prisoner at that! What had Philemon done to him, and why was he not condemned for it by the apostle? Secondly, how can Paul possibly make this unfortunate slave put his head back in the lion's mouth? Thirdly, why does he not subject the evil institution of slavery to a critical analysis?

There is also the further question, of course, whether slavery would have been brought to an end sooner than the nineteenth century in ostensibly Christian countries if Paul had spoken out more aggressively. Possibly it would have achieved nothing; certainly it would not have crossed Paul's mind that we should be reading this tiny scrap almost two thousand years later. On the other hand, maybe Paul's insistence on the equality of all Christians before God necessarily implies the end of slavery.

These are important questions, for they can also be asked of that other institution, with which this book is more directly concerned, the relegation of women in the church to an inferior position.

Conclusion: Did Paul Answer the Question?

Paul may not be quite the enemy to women that some have supposed. Certainly he holds the view that in Christ, men and women are equal, and he takes it for granted that women will have leadership roles in the church. He can use of them language that he uses of his male colleagues, including the exalted term "apostle." It is even possible that he was happily married.

At the same time, however, we have seen why the material we shall be looking at in chapter 9 might have seemed a faithful and organic development of Paul's thought for the slightly changed situation of the later first or early second centuries. Moreover, it must be admitted that the question of the status of women was not foremost in his consideration, partly, perhaps, because he thought that everything would quite soon be coming to an end. It would never have occurred to him that centuries later people would be using his letters, written with a particular audience and a particular occasion in view, to legislate about the status of women.

One also has the impression with Paul that he was writing in something of a hurry, which does not help an author to gaze into the future. We have seen, too, that he is slightly hesitant in his treatment of the topic in the important first letter to the Corinthians, perhaps because he had women opponents in Corinth whom he was trying to shout down or possibly because too radical an approach might have damaged the church's missionary activity. All these things may help to explain why Paul's successors wrote in his name the rather more repressive material that we shall be looking at in the next chapter.

That may not seem a very great deal to have emerged from so many pages, but possibly that is because we were asking the wrong question of him. What mattered for him was Jesus Christ, in whom all are one, whether Jew or Greek, slave or free, man or woman. Perhaps that is enough for us to build on.

CHAPTER NINE

THE HOUSEHOLD CODES

NOW AT LAST WE CAN TURN TO THOSE PASSAGES which for our purposes are the most awkward in the New Testament. They are known as "household codes" because they lay down principles for the conduct of a Christian household, perhaps out of a desire for permanence and stability in the context of Graeco-Roman society. Most of them are attributed to the apostle Paul, and as we indicated in the last chapter, there were aspects of his teaching that might have led his successors to suppose that they were interpreting him faithfully in the changed situation of the developing Christian church a generation or two after his death. None of them, however, is demonstrably from the hand of Paul.

Strictly speaking, the term "household codes" refers primarily to those passages in our collection that analyze the rights and duties of three "pairs" of groups in society, namely husbands and wives, parents and children, and masters and slaves. Notice how the "top dog" in each of these pairs is going to be the (male) head of household; notice, too, that in each of the passages that we shall look at, the authors assume that society is patriarchal in the sense that we have indicated and that it is going to remain so. The husband is the senior partner, parents dominate children, and slave masters are in charge of slaves. For many feminist scholars this means that the very existence of these texts is a betrayal of Jesus' original notion of a "discipleship of equals."

A) COLOSSIANS AND EPHESIANS

We can start by looking at two of the most complete of these "household codes," those found in Colossians and in Ephesians.

167

Many scholars nowadays would say that these epistles were written, not by Paul himself, but by a disciple of his in the next generation. As you will see if you compare the two texts side by side, Ephesians seems to have been composed on the basis of the passage in Colossians; this indicates at least that it is later than Colossians.

Colossians 3:1—4:1

Ephesians 5:21—6:9
Be *subordinated* to one another in the fear of the Lord,

Women, be *subordinated* to your men, as is fitting in the Lord.

women to their own men, as to the Lord, because the man is the head of the woman just as Christ is the head of the church. He is the savior of the body. But as the church is *subordinated* to Christ so the women to their men in every respect.

Men, love your women, and don't be embittered against them.

Men, love your women as Christ loved the church and handed himself over on her behalf, so as to consecrate her, purifying her by a washing of water by a word, so that he might present the church to himself as glorious, having no spot or wrinkle or anything like that, but might be holy and unblemished.
So the men ought to love their own women, as loving their own bodies. The one who loves his own woman loves himself, for no one ever hates his own flesh, but feeds it and takes care of it, just as Christ does the church. For we are limbs of his body. Because of

this a person will leave father and
mother and will join on to his
wife, and the two will turn into
one flesh. This is a great mystery.
I am referring it to Christ and to
the church. But now each of you
individually, let him love his own
woman just like himself; and I
want the woman to have reverence for her man.

Children, *obey your parents*
in everything, for this is
pleasing in the Lord.

Children, *obey your parents,* for
this is just.
Honor your father and mother,
which is the first command with
a promise, "that it may be well
for you, and you may have a long
time in the land."

Fathers, don't make your
children bitter, so that they
don't get depressed.

And, fathers, don't enrage
your children, but nourish them
in discipline and in the teaching
of the Lord.

Slaves, *obey* in every respect
those who are your lords in
the flesh not in eye slavery
but in simplicity of heart
reverencing the Lord.

Slaves, *obey* in every respect
those who are your lords in
the flesh
in *reverence* and trembling,
in simplicity of heart
as though you were obeying
Christ not in eye slavery or trying
to please humans but as Christ's
slaves, doing the will of God
from your heart, with a

Whatever you do, work
from your heart as for
the Lord and not for humans,

good will offering slavery as to
the Lord and not to humans,

knowing that from the Lord
you will receive the reward of
the inheritance. To the Lord
Jesus Christ be slaves. For
the one who commits injustice
is repaid his injustice

knowing that if each of us does
anything good, this is counted
by the Lord
(whether you are a slave or free).

And you, slave lords, do the same
to them.
Give up threats.
Be aware that their Lord
and your Lord is in heaven
and there is no class
distinction.

and has no class
distinction.

What are we to make of all this? It may be helpful to point out that the Ephesians text is a somewhat confusing passage, in that for much of the time between 5:23 and 5:33 it is not really clear whether the author is talking about the relationship between a man and his wife or the relationship between Christ and the church. It would doubtless have been easier to grasp for the original readers, who had a better idea of the context into which the epistle was being delivered, although one can get the feeling that the author has not quite made up his mind which he was talking about.

It must also be admitted that we are dealing here with a thoroughly patriarchal view of society, which I have endeavored to indicate by italicizing the key-words: "subordinate," "obey," and "reverence" (or "fear"). Both these texts make the assumption that the churches they are addressing are organized in more or less the way that Roman and Greek society tended to expect. Thus, the male head of house is in charge and the rest of the household is seen in relation to him. This is not a "discipleship of equals," but a world in which women are the inferior sex.

It is true that the man is commanded to love the woman; and some Christian commentators, anxious to defend the text, seize gratefully on this fact and refer to what they call "love patriarchalism," by which they mean a system that is still patriarchal, but whose patriarchalism is mitigated by the fact that those in positions of superiority are commanded to *love* their inferiors. There is something in this, and it may well be that it was a revolutionary doctrine in the ancient world, though it is hard to marshal evidence for such a view, so that even this teaching on family life could be presented as transforming the society around them. It is true, moreover, that the world would be a vastly better place if those whom patriarchy casts in the dominant role had always obeyed the command to love.

Indeed, the Ephesians passage carries a few shocks for those people. You might, for example, put yourself in the place of a patriarch sitting in your accustomed place in the house-church where your group of Christians meets each week. This week the letter to the Ephesians is being read out to you. As chapter 6 opens with its instruction to children to honor their parents, suitably backed up by a quotation from the Ten Commandments, you nudge your offspring to make sure that they are listening, only to have them turn and look pointedly at you when the letter continues by instructing fathers not to irritate their children. Then the patriarch sits back again in relief as the slaves are told their place in verses 5 through 8, but even that respite is short-lived, for he finds himself under instruction again, being put on an equal footing with those slaves. One could argue that patriarchy is at least relativized here, as the church responds to the questions of its time and place.

Nevertheless, even a love patriarchy requires that women, slaves and children be placed in inferior roles in which they have no control over their own destiny, at least in theory, and in which they may find themselves being dreadfully abused in one way or another. We need, therefore to let the old pattern of domination and subordination wither away, to be replaced by a system in which all human beings are of equal value. I do not here consider the place of the rest of creation, but the feminist critique would also imply the view that other creatures are not simply ours to do with as we will. This passage is therefore very difficult to read in a way that is acceptable to contemporary ears.

There are various ways of redeeming it. One is to make the point that the earliest Christians, so far as we can tell, expected the endtime to come very soon. In that situation it is not so urgent to analyze the ills of contemporary society as we might suppose today. And when it became clear, as it was clear, for example, to the author of the letter to the Ephesians, that Jesus was not going to return this week or even this century, Christians undoubtedly tended to accommodate themselves to the prevailing norms of society, partly to make the church more attractive to non-Christians and partly for a quiet life—to avoid accusations of social subversion. You may want to argue that Christianity *ought* to be socially subversive, but Christians have not always managed to live out this aspect of their vocation. A further point in defense of the passage is that the issue of the equal status of women, slaves and children was not a question for that generation in the church in the way that it is for us; they had problems of their own to address. We need, moreover, to remember that this was a moment in history in which the church was starting, or at least certain groups in the church were starting (for this may not have been the whole story) to look more like patriarchal households than anything else. Therefore, to treat of the church and the family in virtually the same breath will not have seemed odd or unnatural.

We do ourselves and the text no service, however, if we blind ourselves to the fact that historically these lines have been used to justify marital tyranny, to wink at child abuse and to support the institution of slavery. Slaves in America, as late as the nineteenth century, were even made to listen to texts of this sort to make it clear to them that they were in the position that God had willed for them and that therefore any restiveness on their part was offensive to God. When we pray these texts, we must do so in humility and with a thoughtful air. Indeed, some writers argue that they should not be read in church or preached on except to criticize them. One sad fact that we should not overlook is that they may have actually represented a conservative reaction to the more liberal ideas that were starting to circulate in Graeco-Roman society in the first century.

We may, however, choose to be consoled that the instructions were almost certainly ineffective. For one thing, regulations like this are not written if there is no demand for them; so we can assume that in the churches to which Colossians and Ephesians are addressed there were wives who were not entirely subservient to their husbands, children who may at times have been less than perfectly obedient and slaves who took advantage of their Christian owners. On the other hand, we cannot in the name of God make a virtue of the institution of slavery, nor of parental or marital tyranny, and we need to recognize that the texts I have quoted do tend in that direction.

B) 1 PETER

We need to bear all this in mind as we turn to the next passage, from 1 Peter. We do not know precisely who wrote it. For various reasons, however, it seems unlikely that it was Peter, the leader of the apostles. The context suggests that the group to whom it was written was suffering a certain alienation from the society around them (1:6; 2:12; 3:17; 4:1, 12–17), and it may have been composed in order to encourage these Christians, for reasons now lost to us, to accommodate themselves a little more readily to that society so as to seem less subversive. Like some other Hellenistic religious groupings, Christianity evidently attracted a good many women and slaves, and if persons of that sort rose to positions of influence in the young church, this could well have given rise to insinuations that they represented a threat to civilization as we know it.

The lines that introduce our passage give the setting and raise the question: How do you live in a hostile environment? The text (2:11–17) reads as follows:

> Beloved, I urge you, as people who belong elsewhere and who do not live in your own country, to keep clear of the passions of the flesh which fight against the soul. Have a virtuous lifestyle among the Gentiles so that while they speak against you as people who do *wicked deeds,* as a result of your *noble deeds* they may see and glorify God on the day of visitation.

> Be *subordinated* to every human institution, on account of the Lord, whether emperors or governors, as people sent by him for the punishment of people who do *wicked deeds,* and to commend those who do good deeds. Because this is how God's will is; to do *good deeds* and silence the ignorance of foolish people, as free

people, and not using freedom as a cover for evil, but as slaves of God. *Honor* everybody, love your brothers and sisters in Christ, *honor* the emperor.

Clearly this passage was written with a particular situation in mind. You might perhaps compare the situation of Catholics in England in the late sixteenth century, where the government was attempting, against the wishes of the majority, to eliminate the ancient faith for its own political ends. Catholics had the following options, as far as we can tell: they could be "church papists" and go for outward conformity with the new dispensation, or they could practice their Catholicism quietly without making too much fuss, or they could take active and possibly violent and treasonous steps to return to the old ways. They might have been encouraged in this last step by the Papal bull *Regnans in Excelsis,* which formally deposed Queen Elizabeth. Now at this distance, that document and the encouragement to Catholics to rebel seems to have been a mistake from which English Catholics are only, at the end of the present century, recovering. And one could argue that the same three options were available also for South Africans opposed to apartheid in the years since 1948. Suppose that in both these cases, and in others that you know about, all were agreed that at that time the most extreme option was the best, it would not follow that in our day Roman Catholics should dethrone the present Queen Elizabeth, nor that in the coming century, those opposed to the South African government should resort to violence. Similarly, the teaching of 1 Peter has a particular situation in view, and we need to analyze our own situation to ask whether the teaching is appropriate for it. To say that the Bible is the Word of God is not to say that we should suspend our God-given intellects when we read it. In reading the text itself, notice that it is not, strictly speaking, a household code since there is in it nothing at all about children or slave masters (though there is a great deal of teaching about slaves) and very little about husbands. Presumably we must think of this as addressed to a church composed largely of slaves and women, or a church in which the behavior of these two groups was seen to be problematic.

First, there is a piece about slaves (2:18–25):

Slaves, be *subordinated* in all *reverence* to your masters, not just the good and decent ones, but also those who are difficult. For this is a grace, if because of an awareness of God someone bears pain while suffering unjustly. There is no glory if you endure patiently being beaten after you have done *wrong;* but if you *do good* and still suffer and endure patiently, this is a grace from God....[There follows a meditation on Christ as Suffering Slave, patterned largely on Isaiah 53.]

Then the wives are treated (3:1–6):

Similarly, women, [be] *subordinated* to your men, so that even if some do not obey the word, because of their wives' *lifestyle* they can be won over without your having to say a word, when they see your chaste and *reverent lifestyle.* So let it not be external, with braided hair and putting gold things everywhere, their adornment; but the hidden self of the heart in the immortality of a gentle and peaceful spirit, which is precious before God. [The clumsiness of this sentence is largely in the original!] So in the old days holy women who hoped in God used to adorn themselves, *subordinating* themselves to their own men, as Sarah *obeyed* Abraham, calling him her Lord, Sarah whose daughters you are, if you *do good* and do not *fear* anything alarming.

Lastly, husbands are (briefly) addressed (3:7):

Similarly, men, live according to knowledge, giving the *honor* appropriate to a weaker one, your womanly vessel [this clause defies translation]; they are fellow heirs of yours in the grace of life, so that your prayers are not obstructed.

What can we say of all this? Firstly, it was clearly written by a man, with its unsympathetic references to women's makeup and the allusion to woman as the "weaker vessel." Once again, notice the key words, which I have italicized: the concern with subordination, and with reverence (the word that can also be translated as "fear"), and with the contrast between good and evil deeds.

As you try to pray or preach your way through this text, it is important to ask what kind of a situation would have produced it. Both here and in the texts that we shall look at next is the strong concern to keep things as they are. What kind of a society engenders that anxiety? And how should one categorize the instinct not to rock the boat? It could, of course, be cowardice, a refusal to face the challenge that God lays before us; but it may also spring from a sense of having not quite the same goals as those who see radically new possibilities. One may, for instance, admire the mother reported in 2 Maccabees (7:20–29, 41) who encouraged her sons to die a barbaric death, indeed, promised to disown them if they did not submit to the torture, without necessarily feeling that all mothers should behave in precisely the same way.

c) The Pastoral Epistles

Here we will inspect some passages from the so-called Pastoral Epistles (1 and 2 Timothy, and Titus). Few scholars nowadays believe that they were written by St. Paul; most people would date them a good bit later than Colossians and Ephesians, possibly early in the second century. Even less than the texts from 1 Peter are they "household codes," but they are worth including here because their patriarchal stance and view of what is "normal" in society go well with the other texts that we have been reading. The tone suggests that what the author wants is a bit of peace (and we may also doubt whether he is in fact going to get it). The first passage (1 Tm 2:8–15) starts with "therefore" and the antecedent of this very strong logical connective is in verse 2 of the same chapter, where the motive is explicitly stated: "...So that we might live a quiet and peaceful life in complete religious propriety." The threat to peace becomes swiftly apparent:

> I want the men to pray in every place, lifting up holy hands, without any anger or dispute. In just the same way, I want the women to adorn themselves with a modest dress-sense, with chastity and sobriety, not in hairdos, gold, pearls or expensive clothes, but in a way that is appropriate to women who profess religion through

good works. Let a woman learn in peace, in all *subordination;* and I do not authorize a woman to teach, nor to exercise authority over a man, but to be at peace. For Adam was created first, and Eve second. And it was not Adam who was deceived, but the woman, and so she fell into transgression. And she will be saved by childbearing, if she remains in reliability and love and holiness with sobriety. The word is reliable.

Clearly women are seen here as inferior, as needing male guidance, unless they are kept in their place (note the use of the term "subordination") and as finding their proper role only in childbearing. Not that there is anything wrong with motherhood; it is simply that neither now nor in the time when these words were written is motherhood the only appropriate Christian option for women. The most plausible explanation for this passage is, it seems to me, that the women were (as the author sees it) "getting out of hand." You do not stress that women must not study if they have shown no inclination to do so; and if you forbid women to have authority over men, then that implies that there was in the early church a woman or group of women (and very possibly men also) who saw nothing wrong in such an arrangement. So, oddly enough, and no doubt reluctantly, our author provides us with evidence that women exercised a leadership role in the Church that he knew. There is matter to pray over here.

Our next passage (5:1–16) gives instructions about the correct way of handling Christians of various ages and various social standings. It starts, perhaps slightly alarmingly:

Do not rebuke an older man, but invite him, as a father. Treat younger men as brothers, older women as mothers, and younger women as sisters, in all purity. Honor widows who are *pukka* widows. If, however, a widow has children or grandchildren, let them learn religious observance to their own household, and repay their parents, for this is pleasing before God. But the *pukka* widow, who is left alone, has hoped in God, and is persistent in supplication and prayer, night and day, whereas the one who lives for pleasure is in fact dead. Proclaim this, so that they may be above criticism. And if someone does not look after their own, and especially those of the household, they have denied the faith and are worse than an unbeliever. Let a woman not be registered as a widow under the age of sixty. She must be only one man's woman, attested for her good works, that is, by bringing up children, taking in visitors, washing the feet of the saints, providing for those in difficulty and by being a disciple in every kind of good work. Don't allow younger widows, for when they start lusting away from Christ, they want to marry, and they get condemned because they have rejected their pristine faith. And at the same time they are lazy, they study and go around the houses. And they are not just idle, but chatterers and busybodies, talking of inappropriate matters. So I want younger women to marry, bear children, be masters in their house and to give the adversary no chance for abuse. For already some have gone chasing after Satan. If any Christian woman has widows in her family, let her look after them, so that the church is not burdened. And then the church can look after the *pukka* widows.

The author appears to be ranting here; and we must assume that he and his readers knew who was referred to as "chasing after Satan." They might have been women who have disagreed with the author in public or who have gone to the church across the road; we simply cannot tell. Obviously he is worried about what I have translated as "*pukka* widows," the real thing as opposed to the fakes, and anxious that the Christian community at large might have to look after women without resources rather than those in their extended families. Clearly, he has a sense that women are inferior (or, if not inferior, then at least *different,* which is only a short step away) and that they should be looking after the home. And it is possible that one form of behavior from which he is discouraging them is that of talking about religion, which could, from a certain rhetorical stance, be described as being "lazy and busybodying and chattering about inappropriate subjects." So these women may have been (we cannot be sure) discussing theology. Once again, our author hands us rather grudging evidence for an intellectual role for women in the early church.

We can complete our review of 1 Timothy by examining 6:1–2,

dealing with the duties of slaves. I include this passage for complete-
ness, on the grounds that slaves and women are more or less in the
same boat in a society that is patriarchal:

> Any slaves that are under the yoke should think their own bosses
> worthy of all honor, to prevent the name and teaching of God
> from being blasphemed. Those whose masters are also believers
> should not despise them because they are fellow Christians; but
> rather they should act as slaves, because [the masters] who are
> helped by this service are believers and beloved.

It is, you may feel, unlikely that these words were penned by a
slave or by anyone with an understanding of what it was like to be a
slave. The dreadful fact is that Christians have often used this text,
in the name of the gospel of liberation, to stop slaves from resisting
their slavery.

The other two Pastoral Epistles, 2 Timothy and Titus, we can
look at more briefly. As we pass through, we may notice the women
mentioned in 2 Timothy: Lois and Eunice (1:3), Prisca (4:19) and
Claudia (4:21). The first two, though they may have been included
for the sake of verisimilitude, can serve to remind us of the important truth that religion is characteristically passed down by the
women. But the author of 2 Timothy does not take an exalted view
of women, despite their importance in passing on the faith, as our
next passage (3:6-7) makes clear, for it talks of people who

> ...make captive stupid little women who are heaped up with sins,
> led by multifarious desires, always studying, and never able to get
> to the knowledge of the truth.

Once again, we may not be wholly wrong in surmising that these
women had been talking about religion and in consequence rocking
the boat. The same anxiety to keep the ship on an even keel is evident in our two citations from the letter to "Titus" (2:3-7, 9-10),
who is told

> ...to instruct old women to be self-restrained, holy in behavior, not
> slanderers, nor enslaved to large quantities of wine, teachers of

good things, so as to educate the young women in proper behavior, so that they love their men and children and are sober, holy, good home managers, subordinate to their own men, so that God's word should not be blasphemed....

...slaves to be *subordinated* to their own bosses in every respect, to give pleasure and not be contradictory, not embezzling, but showing all good faith, so that they may adorn the teaching of our Savior God in every respect.

Once again, there is a concern here for good order, and it springs, it would seem, from a sense that anything else is bad public relations for the church. The teaching will suffer if church members are seen not to "know their place."

Conclusion

Where and how are the women? Certainly the texts we have been examining presuppose a society that is patriarchal, but we have seen that there may be reasons for this. We do not have to suppose that the Holy Spirit is therefore inviting us to build a society in which men and men alone are in charge, and women, children and slaves must accept their inferior places. Indeed, we have seen that each of the texts contains hints that this might not be the case. We must, however, acknowledge that the history of reading these texts in Christianity gives us much of which to be ashamed; they carry with them the permanent danger that they will be read in the interests of the powerful.

What, then, can we do with these texts in our century and the next? We cannot simply excise them from our Bibles, and create a "canon within a canon." The New Testament is there, and is not going to leave us. There would in any case be an element of cowardice in refusing to face the truth, and the pain that comes with it. That does not permit us, however, to use the teachings that were offered to one particular church in one particular situation to lay down ordinances binding for all Christians in all places and at all times, for example, to the effect that women should not be permitted to study theology or be ministers of the Word in prophesying, preaching or teaching. Presumably no reader of this book would support the institution of slavery, which is clearly envisaged in our passages, and not in any way criticized; if that is the case, then the same reader is logically debarred from using these passages to justify the oppression of women and children.

We may wish to look sympathetically on our author's difficulties. No doubt he would argue that Christianity is not about the status of women, but about the person of Jesus Christ. So all he was trying to do was show his contemporaries that being a Christian did not mean having what his contemporaries and compatriots would have regarded as unsavory ideas about the status of women, children and slaves. Especially in 1 Peter and the Pastoral Letters, the writers are worried about the impact upon non-Christians of subversive doctrines and fear that "the teaching may be blasphemed" for all the wrong reasons. Hence the weary repetition of keywords such as "lifestyle," "obey," "honor," "reverence/fear" (the same Greek word underlies both translations), "good deeds," "bad deeds," and, above all that significant word "subordinate," with its relation to ideas like "good order" and "disorder."

Nevertheless, for all our sympathy, we cannot hide from ourselves the fact that we are talking here about power. In trying to make his Christian society look presentable, the author of each of these passages is in fact laying down or at least commending a power structure that is patriarchal. There can be good reasons for insisting on power; for example, when teaching the young, it is fair to neither the taught nor the teacher to allow that "anything goes" or that authority lies with the loudest mouth. But power is a dangerous idol and desperately attractive, so we must watch ourselves with great care when power is involved. Christians of our time cannot separate ourselves from the death-dealing use that has been made of passages such as those we have been looking at in this chapter. Our gospel must be a gospel of life if it is to be anything at all, and we shall do it no service if our only response to the discovery of injustice is "we mustn't rock the boat."

So the texts are there in our Bibles, but we are not to treat them mindlessly. They are the Word of God, but not in any magical sense that denies the humanity (and hence the prejudices) of the authors who wrote them. They are there to be listened to and reflected upon, to discover what God is saying to us today.

CONCLUSION

WHERE AND HOW ARE THE WOMEN?

ONE OF MY CHILDHOOD MEMORIES is of traveling on railway trains and hearing the wheel-tappers performing their essential but largely unsung job. These men would walk up and down a train that was standing in the station, and bang on the metal wheels with a hammer, to see if it "rang true." If the sound was wrong, then there might be something amiss, and that could lead to a serious accident. Obviously their skill, now presumably superseded, was considerable and of considerable importance; it was closer to art than to science.

There is something of this in our reading of the Bible. We listen to the sound that emerges as we read the texts, and whether it "rings true" to our experience of God and of the church. During the last couple of centuries, historical criticism of the Old and New Testaments has given us new insights into the biblical texts. Scripture scholars have a good deal to tell us about the composition of the documents that make up our Bible, about their origin and background, what they might have meant in their own day, how they function as literature, and something about how they work on us today. It is important that these scholars raise for us questions about and "against" the texts of the Bible.

In particular, these scholars may draw our attention to a flaw in our project of reading the Bible, something about the texts that we had perhaps not noticed and which we neglect at our peril. Feminist scholars ask us to remember that the biblical texts were of their time, and evince a particular outlook that in the course of this book has been described as "androcentric" and "patriarchal." Therefore, when we read the texts, we need to be prepared to discount that outlook in order to get closer to what God may be saying to us at this juncture in the church's history.

What, then, about inspiration? Are these texts not inspired, and if inspired, then immune from error? It is important to remember, and this fact has undergirded all that I have written on the New Testament, that these texts are "different." They have the quality to which we give the name "inspiration." That quality is related to the mood that informs great poetry or great leadership, but its essence is not quite the same. Inspiration has something to do with what the church says is inspired, those texts in which the church sees the portrait of God and of Jesus Christ most accurately delineated. It has nothing to do with protecting the human authors of the texts from their own inaccurate perceptions or cultural prejudices. There is one important further point: there is a reciprocal relationship between the texts and the church. Not only does the church sit in judgment on the texts; the biblical text also challenges the church. So the church is actually subject to Scripture's authority as well as being that which ratifies Scripture as authoritative.

Therefore, both the church and the Bible have a weight that biblical scholars as such do not have. Clearly, it is important to listen to what biblical scholars say, and we can read the texts better for knowing something of the political, social and religious issues of the period when the Bible was being written and the canon formed; but the Bible does not depend for its power on the judgment of scholars. The New Testament texts do succeed in telling us about Jesus and the early church. That is to say, they "work"; they comfort people in their misery and challenge them in their complacency. They work because they manage to express the prayerful insights of the church into the mystery of God revealed in Jesus Christ.

Obviously, the way in which the texts express themselves reflects the mixed motives of those who wrote them. These mixed motives include the church's instinctive tendency to side with the powerful (a tendency that the church shows only because we who are church members share it); but the Spirit of God still speaks in the pages of the Bible, asking probing and uncomfortable questions designed to uncover our mixed motivation. The text has its own inner light that is turned onto us as church, and onto itself as a product of sinful humanity, to show up our shabby pretensions and our threadbare power seeking.

Readers will have noticed my tendency, throughout this book, to "defend" or "save" the New Testament text as not inherently hostile to women, to insist that it is a "word of life" for all. I would claim that the underlying message of the text is that all of us stand as equals before God, and that when we use it to justify our own class interests or to rationalize our own prejudices, we are engaged upon a sinful evasion of the fundamental challenge that God's Word addresses to us. Anyone who denigrates as inferior a particular group of human beings and claims scriptural warrant for doing so, is flying in the face of the biblical message, even though many readers of the Bible have in the past done precisely that. Anyone who tries to lock other human beings, or classes of persons, into a lowly position is doing no more than running from their own insecurities. They should not confuse this with the will of God; it is an oppressive tendency from which they themselves require liberation.

It follows, therefore, that insofar as the church has failed to make full use of the gifts of women, particularly if that failure springs from the perception that women are inferior, it has not been faithful to its Master's example. We have seen that there is nothing in Jesus' practice that justifies the subordination of women, and that even in those texts that seem most angrily to argue for such subordination, there are "whispers of liberation," to which the Spirit is certainly inviting us to listen. The church is the poorer for our failure to make use of women's gifts, and the New Testament, did we only listen to it, is trying to tell us so. Women were always faithfully there in the history of Christianity. Very often their presence has been a challenging breath of fresh air, for they brought to tired prejudices something that was different, a quality that the church needs.

Our Christian ministry has to do with service rather than with power. As disciples of Jesus, we have to stand at the foot of the cross, watching the broken woman and the lonely male disciple who henceforth take the road together. No solution to the problem of the role of women in the church will be found to work that does not take its place on Calvary, where the issue is not domination or subordination, but handing on the Spirit to all who believe in Jesus Christ, both women and men. The church must never tire of working to make of itself the "fellowship of equals" that Jesus clearly intended.

SUGGESTIONS FOR FURTHER READING

Byrne, Brendan. *Paul and the Christian Women*. Homebush, New South Wales (Australia): St. Paul Publications, 1988.

Byrne, Lavinia. *Women at the Altar: The Ordination of Women in the Catholic Church*. Collegeville, Minnesota: Liturgical Press, 1994.

Cannon, Katie. *Katie's Canon: Womanism and the Soul of the Black Community*. New York: Continuum, 1995.

Conwell, Joseph. *Impelling Spirit: Revisiting a Founding Experience: 1539– Ignatius of Loyola and His Companions*. Chicago: Loyola Press, 1997.

Daly, Mary. *Beyond God the Father: Toward a Philosophy of Women's Liberation*. Boston: Beacon Press, 1974.

————. *The Church and the Second Sex, with a New Post-Christian Feminist Introduction by the Author*. New York: Harper & Row, 1975 [1968].

————. *Gyn/Ecology: The Metaethics of Radical Feminism*. Boston: Beacon Press, 1978.

————. *Pure Lust: Elemental Feminist Philosophy*. Boston: Beacon Press, 1984.

Hebblethwaite, Margaret. *Six New Gospels: New Testament Women Tell Their Stories*. London: Geoffrey Chapman, 1994.

Isazi-Dias, Ada Maria and Fernando F. Segovia, eds. *Hispanic/Latino Theology*. Minneapolis, Minnesota: Fortress Press, 1996.

Johnson, Elizabeth A. *She Who Is: The Mystery of God in Feminist Discourse*. New York: Crossroad, 1992.

King, Ursula, ed. *Feminist Theology from the Third World*. Maryknoll, New York: Orbis Books, 1994.

Kwok Pui-Lan. *Discovering the Bible in the Nonbiblical World*. Bible and Liberation Series. Maryknoll, New York: Orbis Books, 1995.

Lee, Dorothy. "Presence or Absence: The Question of Women Disciples at the Last Supper." *Pacifica*, vol. 6, no. 1 (February 1993): 1–20.

Levine, Amy-Jill, ed. *Women Like This: New Perspectives on Jewish Women in the Greco-Roman World*. Atlanta, Georgia: Scholars Press, 1991.

Newsom, Carol A. and Sharon H. Ringe, eds. *The Women's Bible Commentary*. Louisville, Kentucky: Westminster/John Knox Press, 1992.

Oduyoye, Mercy Amba. *Hearing and Knowing: Theological Reflections on Christianity in Africa*. Maryknoll, New York: Orbis Books, 1986.

———. *Daughters of Anowa: African Women and Patriarchy*. Maryknoll, New York: Orbis Books, 1995.

Plaskow, Judith. *Standing Again at Sinai*. San Francisco: Harper & Row, 1990.

Plaskow, Judith and Carol Christ, eds. *Weaving the Visions: New Patterns in Feminist Spirituality*. San Francisco: Harper & Row, 1989.

Ruether, Rosemary Radford. *Sexism and God-Talk*. Boston: Beacon Press, 1993.

Russell, Letty M., ed. *Feminist Interpretation of the Bible*. Philadelphia: Westminster Press, 1985.

Schottroff, Luise. *Lydia's Impatient Sisters: A Feminist Social History of Early Christianity*. Translated by Barbara and Martin Rumscheidt. London: SCM Press, 1995.

Schüssler Fiorenza, Elisabeth. *But She Said: Feminist Practices of Biblical Interpretation*. Boston: Beacon Press, 1992.

————. *A Feminist Commentary*. Vol. 2 of *Searching the Scriptures*. New York: Crossroad, 1994.

————. *In Memory of Her: A Feminist Theological Reconstruction of Christian Origins*. New York: Crossroad, [1983] 1994.

————. *Jesus, Miriam's Child, Sophia's Prophet: Critical Issues in Feminist Theology*. New York: Continuum, 1995.

————, ed. *A Feminist Introduction*. Vol. 1 of *Searching the Scriptures*. New York: Crossroad, 1995.

Society of Jesus. "Jesuits and the Situation of Women in Church and Civil Society" (Decree 14). *Documents of the 34th General Congregation*. St. Louis: Institute of Jesuit Sources, 1995.